LISTEN TO HIM

Listen To Him

A Daily Guide to Scriptural Prayer

David E. Rosage

SERVANT BOOKS
Ann Arbor, Michigan

Book design and cover photo by John B. Leidy
Published by Servant Books,
Box 8617, Ann Arbor, Michigan 48107

ISBN 0-89283-108-1
Printed in the United States of America

To all those friends of Jesus
Who led and guided me into a
More personal
Relationship with him

Foreword

A few years ago we published a little booklet entitled *Speak, Lord, Your Servant Is Listening*, which contains some suggestions and directives for praying with the Word of God. It offers for each day of the year a scripture passage for our prayer of listening.

Speak, Lord was well received by many who were eager to listen to the Lord speaking to them through his Word. Since then we have been frequently asked for a sequel which would offer some norms for entering into a deeper, more personal relationship with Jesus.

Listen to Him is the fruit of our feeble human effort to center on the person of Jesus and to listen more intently to the word he is speaking to us. Its format is similar to *Speak, Lord, Your Servant Is Listening*, but its focus is primarily on the person of Jesus.

Those persons who helped and encouraged me in my efforts are far too numerous to acknowledge, but I know their names are written in the heart of Jesus from which source his blessings will descend upon all of them.

May the Lord accept our efforts and draw many into a deeper and more personal union with him.

Introduction

We spend much of our time in initiating, maintaining and enriching relationships with one another. Our primary goal, however, should be to establish a more intimate and a more personal relationship with Jesus. Jesus himself said: "I call you friends" (Jn 15:15). If Jesus wants to be our friend, and if we want to know him as a friend, we must get to know him as a person. Only then can we deepen our friendship with him.

When the first disciples approached Jesus, they asked: "Rabbi, where do you stay?" They were not concerned about what sort of shelter Jesus was living in. They were concerned about what he was teaching, what he stood for. They had heard the message of John the Baptist; now they wanted to learn more from this Prophet whom John called the "Lamb of God."

Jesus' reply to their question was simple and direct: "Come and see." Jesus did not offer them a manual of Christian living. When he said "Come and see," he was inviting them to walk with him, to listen to his teaching, to observe his lifestyle and to accept his challenge to follow him.

Jesus invited them: "Learn from me, for I am gentle and humble of heart" (Mt 11:29).

Jesus encourages us as well to "Come and see." He wants us not simply to know about him and what he taught, but to know him as a person, one who is single-hearted in doing the Father's will, who heals because he loves, who is deeply concerned about the poor, the sinners, the tax collectors and the outcasts, who loves both friend and foe, rich and poor, young and old, Jew and Gentile.

We cannot know a person unless we have listened to that person. We may hear the words a person is speaking, but that is not sufficient. We must listen to him.

Listening means putting ourselves in his or her position, trying to feel what he or she is experiencing, striving to see through his or her eyes. Only when we listen to a person in this fashion can we ever get to know him.

We cannot know Jesus unless we listen to him. There is no end of listening to Jesus. Every time we listen to him we discover a deeper dimension, a new facet, of his loving personality. Our contemplation will last for an eternity.

Only when we listen to a person can we say that we know him. Furthermore, we can love only the persons we know.

The conclusion is obvious. We cannot love Jesus unless we know him. We cannot know Jesus unless we listen to him.

Listen to Him offers a scripture passage for each day of the year which should reveal much about the person of Jesus. A dominant theme is suggested for each week of the year along with a daily scripture passage which develops the theme and reveals more about the personality of Jesus.

Occasionally a passage may be suggested a second time for prayer. This repetition will serve to deepen our experience of Jesus and draw us into a deeper, richer relationship with him.

Jesus invites us to listen to his words so that he can make himself better known to us. He would also remind us that listening is praying.

These pages are prayerfully presented with the hope that, with God's blessing and the guidance of the Holy Spirit, they may help many to listen to Jesus, to know him, and to love him.

I

Mary Presents Jesus

Mary Offers Us Jesus

Luke 2:1-20

WHEN MARY COMMITTED herself unconditionally to the Lord, she became the first Christopher (Christ-Bearer). In rapid succession she presented Jesus cloaked in the secret of God's mysterious love to Elizabeth, Zechariah and to Joseph.

Mary's specific role in the economy of salvation is to present Jesus to us and also to lead us into a deeper relationship with him.

In Bethlehem, Mary presents Jesus to us as a helpless babe, fragile, dependent, needy, vulnerable. The whole scene is surrounded with mystery—the mystery of God's love. God comes in weakness. His power is love, and love is always vulnerable.

The angel invites the shepherd with this announcement: "This day in David's City a savior has been born to you, the Messiah and Lord." The response of the shepherds is one of faith: "Let us go over to Bethlehem and see this event which the Lord has made known to us." How graciously God rewarded that faith. They were able to penetrate that mystery of love: "Once they saw, they understood."

Mary invites us to pause, to contemplate, so that we might understand the mystery of her Son.

The astrologers persevered through all the difficulties and hardships of travel with an enduring faith based on the flimsy evidence of a twinkling star. Nothing could discourage them. Our loving Father rewarded their courageous pursuit with this brief but happy ending: "They found the child with Mary, his Mother" (Mt 2:11). Mary was delighted to present her Child to the unredeemed Gentile world. These astrologers openly professed their faith. "They prostrated themselves and did him homage. They opened their coffers and presented him gifts of gold, frankincense and myrrh" (Mt 2:12).

Mary not only presented her Son, but she also accepted the gifts of the astrologers in the name of her Son. These gifts acknowledged him as Lord. In their loyalty to Jesus, "they went back to their country by another route."

"This Is My Beloved Son"

AS OUR MOTHER, Mary presents her Son to us. She invites us to do as she did: "Mary treasured all these things and reflected on them in her heart." In the quiet time of prayer, the mystery of divine love begins to unfold. Only in prayer can we come to know him.

First Day
Isaiah 7:10-16   *A promise and prophecy.*

Second Day
Luke 1:26-38   *God's plan begins to unfold.*

Third Day
Luke 1:39-56   *A secret shared and confirmed.*

Fourth Day
Luke 2:1-20   *Love is vulnerable.*

Fifth Day
Matthew 1:18-25   *The pain of formation.*

Sixth Day
Matthew 2:1-12   *Rejoicing with great joy.*

Seventh Day
Matthew 2:13-18   *Rejection and flight.*

Additional scripture readings:
John 1:1-18, John 3:16, Galatians 4:1-7

Mary Presents Jesus To Us

Luke 2:22-52

WHEN MARY AND Joseph brought the Child Jesus to present him to the Lord, it was not an empty ritualistic ceremony. It was not merely fulfilling the Law of the Lord. For them it was a total oblation of Jesus to the Father and also an oblation of themselves.

Having been formed by the Holy Spirit throughout her tender years, Mary understood the purpose of the coming of Jesus into the world. This presentation was the formal beginning of his life dedicated solely to his Father's will.

At this ceremony Mary also offered herself to God in whatever capacity she could fulfill her role in his divine plan. Simeon prepared Mary for her role: "You yourself shall be pierced with a sword."

Each day Mary committed herself anew to God's plan. Mary did not yet know about the exile into Egypt, the poverty of Nazareth, nor what Calvary had in store for her.

What joy must have filled her heart, nonetheless, since she was privileged to present her Son to a world awaiting redemption!

Twelve years later, Mary brings into sharp focus two attitudes of Jesus. With maternal concern she would point to them for our imitation.

Jesus was always single-hearted. Only one thing was important to him: to do his Father's will at all times. This was his first priority. This was Jesus' determination throughout his whole earthly life. Even though this separation might cause his Mother some pain, he had to remain in the Temple to touch some lives according to his Father's plan. Mary understood when Jesus said: "Did you not know I had to be in my Father's house?"

Mary also presents her Son as obedient, not only to God, but also to them. "He went down with them, and came to Nazareth, and was obedient to them." Mary presents the Creator of the universe as willing to be obedient to his creatures. What humility, what docility, what mystery!

Here Am I, Lord

OUR GOAL IN life is to continue to die to self and thus to surrender more completely in love to God. Jesus calls us to this end by inviting us to follow in his footsteps. By his word and by his example he clearly mapped out the pathway for us to follow. We will discover that way in prayer.

First Day
Luke 2:22-24   Gift to the Father.

Second Day
Luke 2:25-40   Gift to two holy souls.

Third Day
Luke 2:41-52   Gift of wisdom to the teachers.

Fourth Day
Matthew 2:19-23   A virgin shall conceive.

Fifth Day
Mark 10:35-45   No greater gift.

Sixth Day
John 10:14-18   Earthly life for eternal life.

Seventh Day
Matthew 26:26-30   Total oblation.

Additional scripture readings:
Matthew 5:23-26, Matthew 20:20-28, 1 Peter 2:21-25

Jesus Is the Word

John 14:23-26

GOD LOVES US so very much that he wants to stay in communication with us. In the Old Testament God spoke directly to some privileged men and through them to his chosen people and also to us.

In the New Testament Jesus is the Word of God. The mediation of God's word through angels and prophets gives way to the Word Himself. Mary believes the word which is spoken to her by the angel. The word is also spoken to John the Baptist as to the prophets of old. Nowhere is the word spoken to Jesus, because he himself is the Word speaking to us.

Jesus speaks the Word with light to reveal and also with power to effect. His Word is light which reveals the infinite love with which the Father loves us. In his Word he makes known his own immutable love for us.

His Word reveals the kingdom which he came to establish. His Word invites us to become members of his family. He tells us that he is the Way.

His Word has power to work miracles which are the sign of his kingdom. His Word has power to forgive, to heal, to comfort and console. Jesus as the Word delegates his power to his apostles to continue the establishment of his kingdom.

Jesus is the Word who challenges us as we confront his Word. He challenges us to listen, to accept, to understand and to keep it. He promises us: "Blest are they who hear the word of God and keep it" (Lk 11:28).

One of the most important fruits of his Word is the fact that it reveals to us who Jesus is. We cannot really know Jesus with our hearts except as he makes himself known through what he says and does. Not only do we get to know Jesus as a person, but we shall be united with him for all eternity. If we listen to his word, he assures us: "I solemnly assure you, the man who hears my word and has faith in him who sent me possesses eternal life" (Jn 5:24).

Jesus Present in His Word

THE WORD OF Jesus inspires, motivates, converts and transforms. As we listen, his word finds a home in our heart. There it is operative without our even being aware of it at times. If we are open and receptive to his word, it brings us peace and joy. Listening is loving. Listening is praying.

First Day
John 1:1-5   *His Word is a divine presence.*

Second Day
Mark 1:21-22   *His Word has power.*

Third Day
John 14:23-26   *His Word lovingly received.*

Fourth Day
John 15:3   *His Word cleanses.*

Fifth Day
Luke 11:27-28   *Happiness is listening.*

Sixth Day
Luke 8:4-15   *His Word grows in us.*

Seventh Day
Matthew 7:24-27   *His Word confronts us.*

Additional scripture readings:
Luke 9:35, John 3:31-36, Mark 4:33-34

Jesus Sows His Seed

Mark 4:1-20

BE WITH JESUS as he takes his place in a boat a little off shore so that the huge crowd might see and hear him. Try to experience what Jesus must have felt as his eyes swept over the large assembly of people so eager to hear his word. Take your place on the shore to listen to what Jesus is saying.

In this parable Jesus is enunciating an essential condition for receiving his word. He is using a picture which all his hearers would recognize. As Jesus was talking the people might even have been able to observe a farmer sowing his seed on the fertile slopes surrounding the lake.

Jesus reveals very much about himself in this teaching. ''The seed is the word of God.'' Jesus is that Word. The seed is the divine life which he has come to share with us. How he longs to plant it in our hearts if only we are receptive. Jesus loves us so much that he wants to divinize us by sharing his resurrected life with us.

His love is so great that he wishes to be closely united with us, but he will not force himself upon us. He respects our free will. How vividly he explains the various levels of receptivity as he paints this picture of the farmer sowing his seed and the various conditions of the soil which receives the seed. As Jesus explains this parable, he is pleading with us to ascertain what is our level of receptivity to his word.

How easily we could be influenced by the polluted atmosphere of materialism and humanism enveloping us. Thus unwittingly we may be trampling the seed along the pathway of life. Likewise our response to his love might be enthusiastic at times but our ability to sustain and persevere in our efforts might be wanting. Again the thorns and briars of daily preoccupations might be choking off the influx of his divine life and love.

His word has the power to cleanse, to mold and to transform. It has the power to elicit a gracious, generous, loving response from us if we permit it to do so.

I Have Stilled and Quieted My Soul

WE CANNOT LOVE God if we do not know him. We cannot know him unless we have learned to listen to him in the quiet of our hearts. How wisely the Lord speaks to us through the psalmist: "Be still and know that I am God," and also, "Wait in patience and know that I am God."

First Day
I Samuel 3:1-10   Your servant is listening.

Second Day
Matthew 13:4-23   How well have I listened?

Third Day
Luke 9:28-36   A unique confirmation.

Fourth Day
John 4:34-38   How important to listen.

Fifth Day
Mark 4:21-25   Listen carefully.

Sixth Day
Luke 8:19-21   Listening establishes a relationship.

Seventh Day
James 1:19-25   Listening leads to action.

Additional scripture readings:
John 18:19-20, John 10:14-16 and 27

II

Beatitudes

Poor in Spirit

Matthew 5:3

IN HIS INAUGURAL discourse, Jesus set forth the Beatitudes as the guidelines for all Christian living. In proclaiming this program in the Beatitudes, Jesus was also revealing very much about himself. In effect, he was saying, "I am poor in spirit; blessed will you be if you are poor in spirit."

The blessedness of which Jesus speaks is that deep, quiet, peaceful joy which only God can give. Jesus assures us that no one can take it away from us. It is completely untouchable. It is that joy which at times shines even through our tears. Sorrow and loss, pain and grief, cannot rob us of this joy. Jesus is concerned that we have this joy: "All this I tell you that my joy may be yours and your joy may be complete" (Jn 15:11).

An essential condition for enjoying this kind of blessedness is the genuine poverty of spirit as stated in the first Beatitude. Jesus requires his followers to be interiorly detached from all things whether they possess these goods or not. The more abject our poverty, the more totally can we abandon ourselves to God and the more limitless will be our confidence in him.

Jesus is speaking not merely about material poverty. The Beatitude may be restated: "Blessed is the man who has realized his own utter helplessness and who puts his whole trust in God." This kind of poverty detaches us from terrestrial things and attaches us more completely to God. God means everything to us when we are truly poor in spirit. God is the number one priority in our lives. Our focus is ever riveted on him.

This tenet of Christianity, like so many others, is diametrically opposed to what the world would have us think. Jesus knew that it would not be easy to live this poverty of spirit since we are so enmeshed in the materialistic philosophy of our day. Our thinking is still pelagian. We pride ourselves on our own self-sufficiency. This attitude is antithetical to the revelation Jesus is making of himself in this Beatitude.

Matching Footsteps

JESUS LIVED THIS Beatitude perfectly. He never asks us to do anything which he himself has not already done. In the following scripture passages Jesus will show us how totally dependent he was on his Father and how concerned he was to do the Father's will at all times. Thus he shows us the way. All he asks of us is to follow him so closely that we can be identified with him. That is what it means to be a disciple.

First Day
Luke 4:14-30   Messiah of the poor.

Second Day
Matthew 13:54-58   Just a carpenter's son.

Third Day
Matthew 8:18-22   Even the birds and foxes have more.

Fourth Day
Mark 10:17-31   Too great a condition.

Fifth Day
Matthew 11:28-30   How welcome are the humble.

Sixth Day
Matthew 21:1-11   He remains a simple, humble, modest king.

Seventh Day
Psalm 22   Prayer of one poor in spirit.

Additional scripture readings:
James 2:1-13, esp. v. 5, Revelation 3:14-22, II Corinthians 8:8-15

Consolation for the Sorrowing

Matthew 5:4

WITH EVERY UTTERANCE which crossed his lips, Jesus gives us a new and deeper insight into the mystery of his loving heart. He did not conceal his disappointment when his own people refused to accept him or listen to his message of salvation.

The pain which Jesus suffered was not wounded pride at failure, nor self-pity. No, he knew that those who refused to believe in him would never enjoy peace and happiness in this land of exile, nor would they "possess eternal life" (Jn 5:24). Furthermore, rejection of Jesus is also rejection of his Father. This, too, caused him much pain.

How patiently and how zealously Jesus appealed to his enemies and all those who would not put their faith and trust in him!

Along the route of his triumphal entry into Jerusalem, Jesus paused to survey the City. With a heart overburdened with sorrow he prayed, "If only you had known the path to peace this day" (Lk 19:41ff).

On another occasion he lamented: "O Jerusalem, Jerusalem. . . . How often have I wanted to gather your children together as a mother bird collects her young under her wings, and you refused me" (Lk 13:34).

During the last days of his earthly life, Jesus met his enemies in the Temple area. In his loving concern for their earthly as well as their eternal happiness, he tried to convince them that he was the Messiah. He tried to reason with them to no avail. Their hearts and minds remained closed.

As true disciples of Jesus, we, too, must be concerned about the lack of response to the outpouring of his love upon the world today. Our hearts must be filled with sorrow as we reflect upon the indifference and the outright rejection of Jesus and his message. As we sacrifice, suffer, and pray for them we bring much consolation to the heart of Jesus. We will then be blessed because our hearts are in tune with his heart.

Sorrowing with Jesus

AS WE SPEND time in quiet listening, we can hear Jesus lamenting: ''Come, all you who pass by the way, look and see whether there is any suffering like my suffering.'' We realize that he is lamenting and thirsting for the hearts and souls of men. That we might empathize with him and yearn more deeply to bring others to him, let us pray.

First Day
Matthew 5:4   Grieving with Jesus.

Second Day
Luke 13:34-35   Jesus laments.

Third Day
Luke 19:41- 44   And Jesus wept.

Fourth Day
John 16:20-28   Sorrow will be turned into joy.

Fifth Day
John 12:44-50   Faith in Jesus is faith in God.

Sixth Day
John 19:25-27   Mary at the cross.

Seventh Day
II Corinthians 1:3-7   God himself comforts us.

Additional scripture readings:
*Lamentations 1:12, Acts 5:17- 41, Hebrews 12:1-13,
James 4:1-10, Matthew 26:36-46*

Meekness

Matthew 5:5

IN THIS BEATITUDE, as in all the others, Jesus was saying in effect: "I am lowly, and blessed will you be if, like me, you are lowly." In telling us what he was like, Jesus singled out the virtue of meekness: "I am gentle and humble of heart" (Mt 11:29).

No other virtue makes us more Godlike than meekness. If we are meek we are already making some progress on the pathway to holiness. Meekness is complex. When we are meek, we have a mastery over ourselves which helps us to restrain the impulses to anger. We are patient, and tolerant of others and ready to forgive.

Certainly Jesus was meek and humble of heart. His apostles were slow to believe and understand him and his mission, yet it did not disconcert or exasperate him. He patiently explained again and again.

Jesus was always meek toward sinners. At the moment a sinner showed any signs of repentance, Jesus was eager to forgive and heal. To mention only a few to whom Jesus showed meekness: the Samaritan woman, the adulteress, the sinful woman in Simon's house, Peter, the penitent thief on the cross.

When his own people picked up stones to hurl at him, he threw none in return. When the people of his native town, Nazareth, attempted to cast him over the precipice, he did not threaten but quietly walked away.

When his enemies came to arrest him, he could have struck them dead, but he meekly gave himself up like a lamb led to slaughter. Jesus is the Lamb of God and meekness is characteristic of a lamb. Amid the jibes, insults and blasphemies at the foot of the cross Jesus prayed meekly: "Father, forgive them, for they do not know what they are doing."

Jesus points out this special virtue for our emulation: "Learn from me, for I am gentle and humble of heart."

Learn from Me

MEEKNESS BRINGS US to a fuller recognition of our need for God's forgiving, healing love. It makes us realize how much we have to learn. Meekness brings us to a deep awareness that without God we can do nothing. Meekness disposes us to become the good soil thirsting for the gentle rain of God's love which will help us produce a rich harvest.

First Day
Matthew 5:5   Jesus was lowly.

Second Day
Isaiah 53:7-10   Meek as a lamb.

Third Day
Matthew 11:28-30   The meekness of Jesus.

Fourth Day
Luke 1:46-55   Mary's meekness makes her mighty.

Fifth Day
Matthew 5:38-42   Meekness gives strength.

Sixth Day
Colossians 3:12-17   Meekness makes us Godlike.

Seventh Day
Revelation 5:1-14   Worthy is the Lamb.

Additional scripture readings:
Ephesians 4:1-6, Zechariah 9:9, Psalm 37:8-11

Hungering for Holiness

Matthew 5:6

JESUS LONGS TO have us closely and lovingly united with him. He outlines many pathways which will lead us into a deeper personal friendship with him.

In the first place we must desire this personal relationship with him. Listen to his pronouncement: "Blest are they who hunger and thirst for holiness, they shall have their fill." What Jesus means is: "I am holy, and blest will you be if you want to be holy like me."

To hunger and thirst for holiness means to have a strong desire, a longing, to love Jesus and to be open and receptive to all the means of achieving a deeper relationship with him. Jesus is praying constantly for this union.

Holiness consists of permitting Jesus to live in us, filling us with his divine life. By his indwelling, Jesus nourishes and strengthens us, conditions and transforms us. How fervently Jesus prayed that we might be one with him. Jesus set the goal for our striving: "You must be made perfect as your heavenly Father is perfect" (Mt 5:48).

Jesus invites us to "come and see" who he is and what he is like. When he says "come follow me" he does not mean simply to be in his company, but to put on his mind and his heart.

On another occasion Jesus encourages us to learn from him so that we, too, can become "gentle and humble of heart." He shows us how we can become like him. After washing the feet of his apostles he said: "What I just did was to give you an example: as I have done, so you must do" (Jn 13:15).

Jesus promised in this Beatitude that those who hunger and thirst for holiness will have their fill. Again he confirmed that promise: "No one who comes to me shall ever be hungry, no one who believes in me shall ever thirst." And even more: "No one who comes will I ever reject" (Jn 6:35ff). What comfort and joy to know that Jesus is always faithful to his promises.

Taste and See How Good the Lord Is

EXPERIENCING THE LOVE and presence of God in prayer really whets our appetite to hunger and thirst for holiness. Fasting is a form of prayer. It helps us to enter more deeply into a spirit of prayer, which is another step closer to holiness. Listen to Jesus as he invites us into a deeper union with him.

First Day
Isaiah 55:1-13   *How graciously God invites us to come.*

Second Day
Matthew 5:43-48   *Love is the road to holiness.*

Third Day
Luke 18:18-30   *Holiness cannot be bought.*

Fourth Day
John 17:9-26   *Holiness is oneness with Jesus.*

Fifth Day
Matthew 5:6   *Hunger and thirst satisfied.*

Sixth Day
John 6:35-40   *No greater food. No greater promise.*

Seventh Day
John 13:1-17   *Road to holiness.*

Additional scripture readings:
Psalm 34:1-23, Isaiah 49:1-3

Wellspring of Mercy

Matthew 5:7

THE LIFE OF Jesus is an open book for all the world to see. He came to reveal to us that his Father and ours is a merciful, compassionate God. He opened the door for us to see, know and understand the loving mercy of the Father.

In the parable of the prodigal son, Jesus portrays the fathomless mercy of his Father for all of us his children. How often the psalmist and the prophets remind us of the compassionate love of the Father.

On each page of the open book of his life, Jesus manifests his own merciful love. Jesus identifies with his Father: "The Father and I are one" (Jn 10:20). Like the Father's heart, the heart of Jesus is ever overflowing with mercy and compassion.

How pleased Jesus must have been to be accused of being a friend of sinners and tax collectors. Nor did Jesus create the impression that if a sinner fulfilled all sorts of conditions he would condescend to forgive him. On the contrary, Jesus searches out sinners. The conversion of a sinner fills his heart with joy. Did he not say: "I tell you, there will likewise be more joy in heaven over one repentant sinner than over ninety-nine righteous people who have no need to repent" (Lk 15:7).

The outpouring of his mercy reaches a zenith on Calvary's hill. Above the raucous cries of blasphemy, derision, insults and mockery, we can hear Jesus' plea for mercy for his executioners: "Father forgive them; they do not know what they are doing" (Lk 23:34).

What joy Jesus brought to the criminal hanging on the cross near him: "I assure you: this day you will be with me in paradise" (Lk 23:43).

The contrite, humble, trusting disposition of the criminal was all that was important to Jesus. With his dying breath, our Lord poured his merciful love upon him.

Drinking at the Fountain of Mercy

RADICAL DISCIPLESHIP MEANS not only following in the footsteps of Jesus, but emulating him so closely that we can be identified with him. Jesus urges us: "Be compassionate, as your Father is compassionate" (Lk 6:36). Daily we pray, "Forgive us the wrong we have done as we forgive those who wrong us" (Mt 6:12). As we pray with his word our hearts are filled with greater compassion.

First Day
Isaiah 54:4-10   Love is a mystery.

Second Day
John 8:1-11   No condemning! No condoning!

Third Day
Luke 15:1-7   One precious little sheep.

Fourth Day
Luke 15:11-32   Time for celebration.

Fifth Day
Matthew 9:9-13   Whomever I will.

Sixth Day
Matthew 18:21-35   Seven times?

Seventh Day
Ephesians 2:1-10   God's generosity.

Additional scripture readings:
Isaiah 43:25, II Thessalonians 2:15-17

Single-heartedness

Matthew 5:8

JOHN THE BAPTIST was a paragon of single-heartedness. His determination to exalt the Lord is epitomized in his own words: "He must increase, while I must decrease" (Jn 3:30). Nothing, not even death, could dissuade John from preparing the way of the Messiah.

When Jesus appeared on the scene he was totally and unconditionally absorbed in one preoccupation—doing the Father's will without changing a single iota.

In his infancy Jesus was subjected to the rite of circumcision, the presentation in the Temple, the exile in Egypt, the poverty of Nazareth, all because the Father willed it so.

At the age of twelve, when he was found in the Temple after three days of separation from his parents, he gently and lovingly reminded his Mother that his Father's will must be his first priority. What volumes his few words speak: "Did you not know I had to be in my Father's house?" (Lk 2:49).

At the Jordan Jesus' submission to his Father's will is evident. His mission is divinely confirmed by the Father. The divine will and Jesus' acceptance of it continued after his Baptism, for "Jesus was led into the desert by the Spirit to be tempted by the devil" (Mt 4:1).

During his public ministry when the Jews challenged his teaching, especially that he "was speaking of God as his own Father," Jesus asserted his single-mindedness: "I am not seeking my own will but the will of him who sent me" (Jn 5:30).

What more convincing evidence of Jesus' singleness of purpose than his urgent prayer and then full acceptance: "My Father, if it is possible, let this cup pass me by. Still, let it be as you would have it, not as I" (Mt 26:39).

Thy Will Be Done

JESUS NEVER ASKS us to do anything which he himself has not done. Did he not say: "What I just did was to give you an example: as I have done, so you must do" (Jn 13:15). These words apply to Jesus' whole life. Just as in the Garden of Gethsemane Jesus was strengthened in prayer, so our prayer will enable us to say our continuous "Yes" to the Father.

First Day
Luke 2:41-52   In his Father's house.

Second Day
John 4:31-38   Divine nourishment.

Third Day
John 5:19-30   The work of the Son.

Fourth Day
John 6:35-40   What comfort in the Father's will.

Fifth Day
John 10:25-38   Two wills blended into one.

Sixth Day
John 15:9-17   Loving obedience.

Seventh Day
Luke 22:39-46   Faithful to the end.

Additional scripture readings:
II Corinthians 1:19-22, Philippians 2:5-11,
Hebrews 5: 1-10, Matthew 18:10-14, Luke 10:21-22

Peacemakers

Matthew 5:9

PEACE IS CERTAINLY the characteristic of the messianic age. Jesus came into the world as the Prince of Peace. He came to establish his reign of peace in the world by filling the hearts of all men with his peace, provided they were open to receive this treasured gift.

Peace is the fruit of love. Jesus said: "There is no greater love than this: to lay down one's life for one's friends" (Jn 15:13). The very next day Jesus proved his love by laying down his life, "making peace through the blood of his cross" (Col 1:20).

"In his person the incarnate Son, the Prince of Peace, reconciled all men to God through his death on the cross. In his human nature he destroyed hatred and restored unity to all mankind in one people and one body. Raised on high by the resurrection, he sent the Spirit of love into the hearts of men" (Gaudium et spes n. 78).

Jesus came into the world to teach us how to love. When we learn to love we will enjoy that genuine peace of heart which this world cannot give. Peace on earth is born of love for God, for ourselves and for our neighbor. As we reach out in love to others we will become a peacemaker which Jesus declared blessed.

By his death and resurrection Jesus earned that gift of peace for us. How frequently he greeted his apostles after the resurrection with: "Peace is my farewell to you, my peace is my gift to you" (Jn 14:27).

As we become more and more experientially aware of God's infinite love for us, we will enjoy that peace which the world cannot give. As we radiate this love we, like Jesus, will become peacemakers.

Channel of Peace

IN THIS BEATITUDE, peacemakers are called the adopted sons and daughters of God. In the process of this adoption "the love of God has been poured out in our hearts by the Holy Spirit who has been given us" (Rom 5:5). As we open ourselves more and more to the outpouring of his love, we do become a channel of peace to others. To this end we are called. Our prayer will lead us to a greater appreciation of this calling.

First Day
Isaiah 9:1-6   A promise of peace.

Second Day
Luke 2:8-20   Peace on earth.

Third Day
Mark 5:25-34   Freedom, the source of peace.

Fourth Day
Luke 7:36-50   Reconciliation brings peace.

Fifth Day
John 16:29-33   Jesus, the source of peace.

Sixth Day
John 14:27-31   A divine gift.

Seventh Day
Colossians 1:15-23   The price of peace.

Additional scripture readings:
Psalm 85:1-14, Luke 1:79, Luke 8:48,
II Thessalonians 3:16

Paradox of Persecution

Matthew 5:10-12

BY HIS WORDS and by the events of his life Jesus taught us what St. Paul was pleased to call "the complete absurdity of the cross and the power of the cross." The Gospel portrays a whole litany of rejections of Jesus throughout his entire earthly life.

Jesus prepared us for a similar fate if we are going to be his disciples. One of the outstanding qualities of Jesus was his sheer honesty. He left no doubt in our minds what would happen if we were to follow him. He came not to make life easy, but to make us great.

In no uncertain terms Jesus told us: "Remember what I told you: no slave is greater than his master. They will harry you as they harried me" (Jn 15:20).

Jesus assures us of great consolation amid persecution: "I tell you truly: you will weep and mourn while the world rejoices; you will grieve for a time, but your grief will be turned into joy" (Jn 16:20).

To which St. Paul adds: "I consider the sufferings of the present to be nothing as compared with the glory to be revealed in us" (Rom 8:18).

We might ask ourselves why persecution is so inevitable? It is inevitable because the truths which Jesus taught and the kingdom he set up are bound to be the conscience of a nation and the conscience of society. Where there is good, the Church must praise it; where there is evil, the Church must condemn it. Furthermore, the life of the individual disciple of Jesus is often a silent condemnation of the lives of others, and he will not escape their hatred.

Jesus may not ask us to die for him, but rather to live for him, which may be even more difficult. In a special Beatitude Jesus assures us: "Blest are you when they insult and persecute you." And he advises us to "Be glad and rejoice, for your reward is great in heaven" (Mt 5:10ff).

Sign of Contradiction

JESUS REMINDED US that persecution would come in many different ways: barbed remarks, open criticism, sly allusions, total rejection. As we spend time in prayer, we begin to understand that persecution makes us more and more like Jesus. As our love for him grows, we will be able to "be glad and rejoice."

First Day
Matthew 5:10-12   *Joy in suffering.*

Second Day
John 15:18-27   *Together with Jesus.*

Third Day
John 16:20-28   *Grief will be turned into joy.*

Fourth Day
Luke 21:5-19   *Persecution in the last days.*

Fifth Day
Mark 4:1-20   *The power of the word.*

Sixth Day
Matthew 10:5-42   *A disciple's expectation.*

Seventh Day
I Corinthians 1:18-25   *Folly of the cross.*

Additional scripture readings:
John 17:9-19, Romans 8:18-25

Jesus Is Disappointed

Luke 12:22-31

EVERY ONE OF US wants to be loved and accepted by others. In his humanity, Jesus, like us, also wanted to be accepted and loved. However, his desire to be accepted is in no way for his own gratification.

Jesus knew that our acceptance of him and our faith in him would bring us joy and happiness in this life and the certainty of life eternal. Scripture says plainly: "Without faith it is impossible to please God" (Heb 11:6). Without faith we cannot be saved. That is why Jesus always pleaded for faith in him and all that he taught.

How disappointed Jesus was when people refused to believe in him. When his own people in Nazareth refused to believe in him "He could work no miracles there. . . . so much did their lack of faith distress him" (Mk 6:5). On another occasion Jesus appealed to his hearers in these words: "Even though you put no faith in me, put faith in these works" (Jn 10:38).

Jesus was disappointed in his disciples for their lack of faith. When they were threatened by a storm as they crossed the lake, Jesus chided them with: "Where is your courage? How little faith you have!" (Mt 8:26).

When the disciples tried to cast out the devil at the foot of Mt. Tabor and failed, Jesus said: "What an unbelieving and perverse lot you are!" He went on to say: "If you had faith . . . nothing would be impossible for you" (Mt 17:14-21).

On the day of the resurrection Jesus good-naturedly rebuked the disciples on the road to Emmaus: "What little sense you have! How slow you are to believe all that the prophets announced" (Lk 24:25).

On the other hand, how many times does Jesus remind us of the fruits of a dynamic, vibrant, operative faith. "Your faith has restored you to health," and, "I have never found this much faith in Israel" (Mt 8:10). This pleased Jesus. How pleased he is with our faith in him!

I Do Believe

AS THE DISAPPOINTMENT of Jesus comes more into focus in our prayer, we spontaneously begin to examine ourselves about our own faith or lack of faith in him. How pleased Jesus must be when our prayer prompts us to say: "I do believe! Help my lack of trust."

First Day
Luke 17:5-6   *How big is a mustard seed?*

Second Day
Matthew 8:23-27   *Billowing waves threaten.*

Third Day
Matthew 22:15-22   *Simulated faith.*

Fourth Day
Mark 6:1-6   *Lack of faith spells no power.*

Fifth Day
John 10:34-38   *What more could I have done?*

Sixth Day
John 12:44-50   *Faith illumines the way.*

Seventh Day
Hebrews 11:1-40   *Stalwarts in faith.*

Additional scripture readings:
Luke 12:22-31, Matthew 14:22-33, Mark 16:9-14

Who Is Jesus?

Luke 9:18-22

ONE DAY JESUS asked the apostles a very crucial question. At this stage in his public ministry this question was of supreme importance. Jesus challenged the apostles with this searching question: "But you—who do you say that I am?"

Jesus was rapidly approaching the end of his teaching ministry. His death was imminent. It was important that he know whether the disciples really comprehended who he was.

We can well imagine the fleeting anxiety which stirred in the heart of Jesus as he awaited an answer. Did they recognize him for what he really was, or was the popular opinion of the Messiah as a conquering king still uppermost in their minds.

How pleased Jesus must have been to hear Peter declare, "You are the Messiah of God." Yet it was not enough that they recognize him as a teaching, healing Messiah, but that they also understand that he must be the suffering servant as well. "The Son of Man must endure many sufferings." Did they really comprehend that he would be rejected, executed and rise again? This was the price Jesus had to pay for man's sinfulness. It was occasioned by his own people's rejection of him as the Messiah.

Jesus asks us the very same question: "Who do you say that I am?" It is of supreme importance to Jesus that we answer that question for ourselves.

Observe that Jesus waited for the propitious moment to ask this question. The disciples had gone into seclusion with him in the neighborhood of Caesarea Philippi. They had gone there to be alone with Jesus, to reflect, and to pray. It was in this prayerful setting that Jesus asked this all-important question. He did not ask them while he was engaged in his teaching and healing ministry, surrounded by the excitement and distraction of the crowd. Listen to Jesus ask: "But you—who do you say I am?"

Personal Discovery

WHO IS JESUS for me? It is not enough to know about Jesus; we must know him personally. We may be well-versed in Christology and still not know who and what Jesus is. Only in solitude and prayer will we be able to recognize Jesus for what he really is. Only at the core of our being and in the silence of our own heart will we find Jesus. As we pray the answer will come. Verbalize it to yourself and if you have the courage, write it down. The following scriptures will help you recognize Jesus.

First Day
Matthew 16:13-20   *This is a crucial question.*

Second Day
Mark 8:27-30   *A profound discovery.*

Third Day
Luke 4:40-44   *Even demons recognize him.*

Fourth Day
Luke 17:22-37   *The day of the Son of Man.*

Fifth Day
John 10:14-18   *Totally selfless oblation.*

Sixth Day
Luke 24:1-12   *We should have remembered.*

Seventh Day
II Timothy 1:6-14   *Paul "knew" Jesus.*

Additional scripture reading:
Isaiah 52:13 to 53:12

III

Jesus Prays

Jesus' Fidelity to Prayer

Luke 11:1-13

JESUS WAS ALWAYS faithful to prayer. He prayed always and everywhere. Even though he had only a few short years in which to establish his kingdom, he took time out regularly and consistently to spend in prayerful union with his Father. He went off to a mountaintop, a desert place, an olive grove to be alone with his Father. Frequently he invited his apostles to come apart and pray.

Jesus was always in union with his Father, but as a man he wanted to reenforce and deepen that union. He did not merely pray on location, but he sought out quiet places for prayer. He wanted solitude.

St. Luke speaks of the prayer of Jesus with such expressions as: "One day when Jesus was praying in seclusion and his disciples were with him. . . ." (Lk 9:18). Or again: "He often retired to deserted places and prayed" (Lk 5:16). On another occasion the evangelist says: "When he had taken leave of them, he went off to the mountain to pray" (Mk 6:46).

Jesus was also faithful in praying in public. St. Luke puts it this way: "Entering the synagogue on the sabbath as he was in the habit of doing. . . ." (Lk 4:16). Jesus was never too busy to pray.

The whole life of Jesus exposes the fallacy of the excuse we make at times: "My work is my prayer." In spite of his work, Jesus made time for prayer. Jesus' life also exposes the convenient rationalization: "We have no time for prayer." By his example Jesus taught us how relevant, essential and necessary prayer is in our daily living.

Jesus prayed before all the important events of his life. He prayed before selecting his disciples (Lk 6:12). He prayed after long arduous days of teaching and healing.

With the disciples let us not only beg, "Lord, teach us to pray," but also, "Lord, teach us how to be faithful in prayer by giving you the time and effort each day which is rightly yours."

Prime Time

JUST AS REGULAR eating habits and a proper diet are essential to our physical health, so disciplined time and effort in prayer is a prime requisite for our spiritual well-being. Jesus' life encourages and urges us to fidelity in prayer. Accompany Jesus as he goes to prayer and pray with him.

First Day
Luke 4:14-30   Jesus was faithful to the sabbath liturgy.

Second Day
Luke 5:12-16   Jesus retired to pray.

Third Day
Luke 9:18-22   Faith comes through prayer.

Fourth Day
Luke 9:28-36   Prayer has a transforming power.

Fifth Day
Matthew 14:22-23   From the mountain to the sea.

Sixth Day
John 17:9-26   Jesus prays for his disciples and for all believers.

Seventh Day
Matthew 26:36-46   In agony Jesus found solace and comfort in prayer.

Additional scripture readings:
Matthew 6:5-15, Matthew 7:7-11, I Timothy 2:1-8

Gratitude Characterized
Jesus' Prayer

Luke 22:14-20

JESUS WAS ALWAYS deeply grateful to his Father. He paused many times in his ministry to verbalize his gratitude in prayer. Jesus often punctuated his teaching and healing ministry with a prayer of thanksgiving.

When Jesus was about to feed the five thousand, John describes Jesus' action and attitude in these words: "Jesus then took the loaves of bread, gave thanks, and passed them around to those reclining there" (Jn 6:11).

Another important event was the raising of Lazarus to life after he had been dead for four days. Before Jesus called Lazarus forth from the tomb he prayed: "Father, I thank you for having heard me" (Jn 11:41).

How the heart of Jesus overflowed with joy and gratitude when he was about to give us himself in the Holy Eucharist. May his sentiments of gratitude sink into our hearts as he says: "I have greatly desired to eat this Passover with you before I suffer." In recording the institution of the Eucharist the evangelist does not fail to mention the gratitude which filled Jesus' heart: "Then taking a cup he offered a blessing in thanks. . . . Then, taking bread and giving thanks, he broke it and gave it to them." Jesus instituted the Eucharist as the most powerful means we have to express our gratitude to God.

Jesus also teaches us the necessity of thanksgiving in telling us of the ten lepers who were cleansed of this loathsome disease. Listen to the disappointment of Jesus at their lack of gratitude. "Were not all ten made whole? Where are the other nine? Was there no one to return and give thanks to God except this foreigner?" (Lk 17:17ff).

Jesus taught us by his word and by his own prayer life how important is a genuine spirit of gratitude. His whole life was a continuous act of thanksgiving culminating in the solemn act of thanksgiving in the Eucharist.

Thank You, Father

WHEN OUR HEARTS are filled with gratitude, all the pieces of the jigsaw puzzle of life fit together. We recognize and appreciate all the blessings lovingly bestowed upon us by our gracious Father. Such gratitude enables us to use well his manifold gifts. May our reflections on the words of Sacred Scripture deepen our awareness of God's goodness and continue to form us into a humble, grateful person.

First Day
Psalm 138 — *A prayer from a grateful heart.*

Second Day
John 6:1-15 — *First thanksgiving, then the gift.*

Third Day
Matthew 11:25-30 — *In prayer we come to know the Father.*

Fourth Day
John 11:1-44 — *A moment for thanksgiving before the drama.*

Fifth Day
Luke 17:11-19 — *Only ten percent.*

Sixth Day
Luke 22:14-20 — *The perfect act of thanksgiving.*

Seventh Day
Philippians 4:4-7 — *Paul urges prayer full of gratitude.*

Additional scripture readings:
Psalms 145 and 65, Colossians 1:3-14

Yes to the Father

Luke 22:39-46

THE PRAYER OF Jesus was always yes to the Father. His prayer was always a response in love to the Father's love.

Love is expressed in the act of giving. Genuine love gives generously without counting the cost. Mature love finds great joy in giving. Infinite love must give everything.

Love is mutual. It gives and it receives. The most precious gift is the gift of self. It is a union of two wills melted into one, fully in accord with each other. Thus Jesus loved and thus the Father loved him. "The Father loves me for this, that I lay down my life" (Jn 10:17).

Genuine love not only keeps two hearts in tune with each other, but it forges them into one. Did not Jesus say, "The Father and I are one?" How appropriate the words which the psalmist used to describe Jesus' attitude: "To do your will, O my God, is my delight" (Ps 40:9). St. Paul confirms this attitude: "Jesus Christ was not alternately 'yes' and 'no'; he was never anything but 'yes' " (II Cor 1:19).

Jesus told us that we would be blessed if we were single-hearted. He even mapped out the way for us. He was always single-hearted in responding to the Father's will.

Even in the bitter hours of his passion Jesus' prayer was one of full union with the Father's will: "Father, if it is your will, take this cup from me; yet not my will but yours be done. In his anguish he prayed with all the greater intensity" (Lk 22:42-44). And in his dying moments he gives himself totally to the Father: "Father, into your hands I commend my spirit" (Lk 23:46).

In the only formula of prayer which Jesus taught, he instructed us to pray: "Your will be done on earth as it is in heaven" (Mt 6:10). In these words Jesus taught us the ideal prayer-posture: "Here I am, Lord, what is it you want?"

Our Yes to the Father

TO PRAY WELL we must be free from anything which leads us away from God. Some inordinate attachments which make prayer difficult are anger, resentment, adherence to our own ideas, fear of criticism, need for constant approval of others. If our mind is attached, our heart is not free to love and to pray. Linger with Jesus and pray for the same attitude which he had.

First Day
Psalm 40:7-11   His will a delight.

Second Day
John 4:31-38   No food necessary.

Third Day
John 6:37-40   He will not be rejected.

Fourth Day
John 5:19-30   The Father and Son work together.

Fifth Day
Matthew 6:9-13   The perfect prayer.

Sixth Day
Luke 22:39-46   The Father's will at any cost.

Seventh Day
Luke 23:44-49   Final submission.

Additional scripture readings:
Matthew 7:21-23, Matthew 6:25-34, II Corinthians 1:18-22

Jesus' Prayer Was Contemplative

John 15:9-10

JESUS TAUGHT US that prayer should not be a burdensome, exhausting duty, but rather a refreshing, rejuvenating experience. He assured us that if we come to him, he would refresh us.

Jesus prayed contemplatively. By his own example Jesus taught us how to pray this way. When we bask in the sunshine of God's love we are praying. When we pause to let him love us, we are praying contemplatively.

Jesus prayed in this way. The sacred writer says: "Then he went out to the mountain to pray, spending the night in communion with God" (Lk 6:12). This type of union with the Father is prayer at its best. It is refreshing and relaxing.

On another occasion, the evangelist describes Jesus, at prayer, after an evening of healing: "Rising early the next morning, he went off to a lonely place in the desert; there he was absorbed in prayer" (Mk 1:35). This absorption in prayer is a contemplative posture.

Jesus wanted to be alone with his Father. How frequently the evangelists remind us of this fact! "He often retired to deserted places and prayed" (Lk 5:16). Once again we are told: "He went up on the mountain by himself to pray" (Mt 14:23).

Contemplative prayer is loving God and letting him love us. Jesus describes it in these words: "As the Father has loved me, so I have loved you. Live on in my love." Walking, playing, working, living in his love is prayer.

Jesus encourages us in this type of prayer and St. Paul explains why: "All of us, gazing on the Lord's glory with unveiled faces, are being transformed from glory to glory into his very image by the Lord who is the Spirit" (II Cor 3:18). In brief, we become what we contemplate.

Praying Is Loving

CONTEMPLATIVE PRAYER IS loving. When we pray in this fashion our whole being is absorbed in God and his overwhelming love for us. We are not concerned about problem solving, nor in verbalizing our petitions, but rather in loving God and letting him love us. Thus we put on the new man by acquiring the mind and heart of Jesus.

First Day
Job 36:22-23   *The God of awe and reverence.*

Second Day
Mark 1:35   *Total immersion.*

Third Day
Luke 6:12   *No more intimate friendship.*

Fourth Day
Luke 9:28-36   *Listen to him!*

Fifth Day
John 15:9-10   *Living in love.*

Sixth Day
Matthew 6:5-8   *Alone with the Father.*

Seventh Day
II Corinthians 3:12-18   *Molding our image.*

Additional scripture readings:
Matthew 14:22-24, Luke 5:16, Luke 3:21

IV

Jesus Heals

Jesus Personifies God's Healing Power

Matthew 11:2-6

ALREADY IN THE Old Testament our loving Father reminds us that he is our healer. "I, the Lord, am your healer" (Ex 15:26). We readily recall some of the healings in the Old Testament which were wrought through God's healing power: the leprosy of Naaman, the sinfulness of David, the widow of Zarephath and her son, to mention only a few.

When Jesus came into the world, he also wanted to be known as a healer. When a delegation came to him from John to ask him, "Are you 'He who is to come' or do we look for another?" Jesus simply pointed to his healing mission as the proof of his messiahship: "The blind recover their sight, cripples walk, lepers are cured, the deaf hear, dead men are raised to life, and the poor have the good news preached to them" (Mt 11:2-6).

Jesus might have pointed out that all the prophecies were being fulfilled in him as he did to the disciples on the road to Emmaus. Rather he chose to be identified only by his healing mission. He wanted them to recognize him for the compassionate love with which he was reaching out to all the afflicted.

Jesus healed because he had the power to heal. However, he healed not so much to demonstrate his divine power, but primarily to reveal his loving concern and his empathy for all who were suffering. He suffered along with all the afflicted.

There is not a single case on record when Jesus refused to heal. There are some instances when certain persons refused his healing. Furthermore, Jesus healed in every area of human suffering. He always healed the whole person.

"Jesus Christ is the same yesterday, today and forever" (Heb 13:8). His love is unchanging, eternal and infinite. Jesus eagerly continues his healing mission in our midst.

A Wounded People

ALL OF US stand in need of constant healing. Our loving Father is our healer. Jesus came into the world to manifest his healing love and to touch all in need of healing. The only condition he asks of us is that we trust him and confidently open ourselves to his healing power. As we pray with his word, we will become more receptive to whatever he wishes to accomplish in us.

First Day
I Kings 17:7-24   *Generosity rewarded.*

Second Day
II Kings 5:1-14   *Humble submission is blessed.*

Third Day
Luke 5:12-16   *Jesus wills our healing.*

Fourth Day
Luke 4:14-30   *The healer walked away.*

Fifth Day
Luke 7:1-10   *Humble, expectant faith rewarded.*

Sixth Day
Luke 13:10-17   *Even on the Sabbath.*

Seventh Day
Matthew 11:2-6   *Reading the signs.*

Additional scripture readings:
Psalm 51, Luke 5:17-26

Jesus Heals Sinfulness

Luke 7:36-50

IN ALL THE events of his life Jesus demonstrates an everbroadening dimension of his divine love. When he accepted the invitation of Simon the Pharisee to dine with him, Jesus took the occasion to reveal the overwhelming love with which he always reached out to sinner and saint, to young and old, to rich and poor.

Jesus' love is infinite, immutable and universal. The only limitation on his love is the receptivity of the person to whom his love is extended.

"A woman known in the city to be a sinner" approached Jesus with a genuine sense of her sinfulness, but also with a deep awareness of his loving mercy and compassion. She humbly recognized her own wretchedness and poverty of spirit, but the love in her heart assured her that Jesus alone could forgive, heal and redeem.

Jesus did not exact from her any admission of guilt, nor any guarantee of sincerity of conversion. His gentle, merciful love responded to the demonstrative but wordless expression of her love.

In spite of the discourtesy and insult which Jesus received from Simon, he reached out to him with a gracious, genuine, kind, merciful love. When Jesus addressed himself to the Pharisee, it was in these words: "Simon, I have something to propose to you." It was an expression of his loving concern for Simon. It was a firm, but gentle invitation to conversion. Simon considered himself a good man before God and man. His self-righteousness blinded him to genuine love.

Both Simon and the penitent woman approached Infinite Love. How different was their ability and capacity to receive love! The loving heart of the Good Shepherd is always the same—always in search of the lost sheep—always eager to forgive, to heal, and to redeem.

In His Presence

AS WE APPROACH and bask in the sunshine of his presence, we can see ourselves more clearly. In the light of his love we can better assess our own attitudes — be they self-righteous, repentant, trusting, humble, sincere. As we walk in his presence, as we prayerfully listen to the intensity of his love, we will be better enabled to accept his forgiving, healing love and respond to it with greater courage and confidence.

First Day
I Samuel 12:1-25   Am I that man?

Second Day
Luke 15:1-7   Joy in heaven.

Third Day
John 8:1-11   Message in the sand.

Fourth Day
Mark 2:1-12   No partial healing here.

Fifth Day
Luke 18:9-14   Both prayed in the temple.

Sixth Day
Luke 23:34   Zenith of mercy.

Seventh Day
I John 3:4-10   Sinfulness and holiness incompatible.

Additional scripture readings:
Psalm 32, Matthew 9:9-13

Jesus Heals Blindness

Mark 10:46-52

DURING HIS HEALING ministry Jesus was often confronted with blindness. No doubt, physical blindness was a prevalent affliction at the time. However, Jesus frequently encountered spiritual blindness in those who lacked faith in him, or even rejected him and his message of salvation. This caused him much pain.

In dealing with blindness Jesus once again reveals very much about himself, his personality and above all his heart.

When Bartimaeus heard that Jesus of Nazareth was passing by, he knew that Jesus had the power to heal him. In his world of darkness he must have pondered often the marvelous things which he had heard about Jesus. He believed in him. This is evident from the messianic title with which he addressed Jesus: "Son of David." Jesus appreciated this faith in him.

Bartimaeus was persistent in his prayer. "Many people were scolding him to make him keep quiet, but he shouted all the louder, 'Son of David, have pity on me.'" His perseverance also pleased Jesus.

For a time, Jesus was totally unconcerned about the crowd around him and centered all his attention and love upon one person. Each individual is precious to Jesus. Bartimaeus's plea must have touched the heart of Jesus: "Rabboni, I want to see!" For the benefit of the crowd and for us, Jesus said: "Your faith has healed you."

How often Jesus encounters spiritual blindness! This appears at times as a lack of faith, or a refusal to believe or outright rejection of him. How chilled Jesus is at this failure to believe! Yet his great love dominates this rejection. He continues to reach out in patient, forgiving love. Only God could love so deeply.

Honing Our Vision

OUR OWN VIEW is often myopic. Our horizon is often so limited. How often we are shortsighted, self-centered, fearful, doubting. Jesus' action and attitude in meeting blindness can be a great source of inspiration and encouragement to us. May our continuous prayer be: "Rabboni, I want to see."

First Day
Mark 10:46-52 *Seeing through blindness with the eyes of faith.*

Second Day
Matthew 9:27-31 *Faith gives power.*

Third Day
Mark 8:22-26 *Jesus helps put our vision in focus.*

Fourth Day
Luke 6:36-49 *A speck and a plank.*

Fifth Day
Matthew 23:13-39 *Jesus decries spiritual blindness.*

Sixth Day
II Peter 1:3-11 *Short-sightedness leads to blindness.*

Seventh Day
John 9:1-41 *Physical and spiritual blindness.*

Additional scripture readings:
Luke 18:35-43, Matthew 20:29-34, Matthew 15:1-20

No Limitation on Jesus' Healing

Mark 1:32-39

JESUS HEALED ANYONE who came to him. He healed because he loved every person, recognizing in each one an adopted child of the Father. His empathy was so great that he could not tolerate suffering of any kind. His love is universal; no one is excluded. His healing love touched all people, his own people first, then Gentiles (e.g., the Canaanite woman's daughter, Mk 7:24f), even his enemies, (e.g., Malchus, Lk 22:51).

Secondly, Jesus healed because he had the power to heal. He healed all physical and psychological as well as spiritual ills. Jesus not only healed certain maladies, but he always healed the whole person. He also had power over life and death.

The love and power of Jesus not only healed individuals, but it healed whole groups of people. Luke says: "At sunset, all who had people sick with a variety of diseases took them to him and he laid hands on each one of them and cured them" (Lk 4:40).

As Jesus went about his healing mission, he taught us a valuable lesson on prayer. Jesus always approached any healing prayerfully. Likewise, he never failed to thank his Father after a healing session.

Frequently Jesus would escape to a mountaintop or a desert place to reflect, to pray, to thank and praise the Father for permitting him to manifest this healing love so extensively and so intensely. St. Mark records such an event. "After sunset, as evening drew on, they brought him all who were ill and those possessed by demons" (Mk 1:32ff). It must have been an exhausting night; nevertheless, Jesus wanted to be alone with his Father. Mark goes on: "Rising early the next morning, he went off to a lonely place in the desert; there he was absorbed in prayer."

Quietly but effectively Jesus teaches us that prayer is a fruitful channel of healing. Furthermore, prayerful gratitude makes us even more receptive to ongoing healing.

I, the Lord, Am Your Healer

JESUS TEACHES US that there is no limitation to his healing love and his power to heal. A necessary condition for receiving his healing is to be open and receptive and to seek his healing with confidence and trust. As we contemplate his many and various healings we become more open to what he wishes to effect in us. A frequent "Lord, heal me" disposes us to his healing love and power. Be with Jesus as he heals.

First Day
Luke 8:26-39   *The devils and the swine.*

Second Day
Mark 9:14-29   *Prayer and fasting are essential.*

Third Day
John 5:1-15   *After thirty-eight years.*

Fourth Day
Luke 8:40-56   *Jesus is sensitive to a young girl's hunger.*

Fifth Day
Luke 7:11-17   *Listen to Jesus say, "Do not cry."*

Sixth Day
Mark 2:1-12   *No obstacle insurmountable.*

Seventh Day
Luke 5:12-16   *A healing touch.*

Additional scripture reading:
Luke 7:1-10

Group Healings:
Matthew 8:16-17, Mark 1:32-34, Luke 4:40-41

Jesus Extends His Healing Power

Luke 9:1-6

JESUS HEALED WHEREVER he went. His heart was filled with compassion for all those who were suffering in any way. Humanly speaking his time and efforts were limited. He could cover only so much territory. To extend his healing mission and to relieve more suffering, Jesus did something unusual.

Jesus had called the Twelve in order to instruct and teach them, to form and transform them, so that they might become the pillars upon whom he could build his Church after he left this world. During this period of formation, he did not commission or empower them to begin their apostolates with only one exception.

His heart yearned to relieve pain and suffering in many towns and villages which he could not reach. Therefore, prematurely, as it were, he gave the Twelve "power and authority to overcome all demons and to cure diseases."

The apostles went out to heal by preaching the good news, by laying on of hands and by anointing with oil. Thus they became the extension and the personification of Jesus to many of the sick.

Jesus' love is everlasting and universal. He knew that because of the sinfulness of our human nature, we, too, would need healing. For this reason he established his Church as a healing Church. Jesus instituted some special channels of healing which we call sacraments.

The Sacrament of Baptism heals us by bridging the chasm between us and God. By uniting us with the divine life which he shares with us, we become the temples of the Holy Spirit in Baptism. The anointing of the sick is obviously a healing sacrament.

By his overflowing mercy Jesus forgives and heals us in the Sacrament of Reconciliation. By his presence and his power Jesus heals in the Holy Eucharist.

Love will always find a way, and Jesus is that way.

Healing Presence

WE ARE A pilgrim people. We are a sinful people. In spite of our waywardness, Jesus is dwelling with us and within us. By his healing presence he is continuing his redemptive work among us. What joy we give him when we humbly and confidently beg for the outpouring of his healing, forgiving love. As we contemplate his word we can better see our need and more readily open ourselves to his healing love.

First Day
Ezekiel 36:25-28   A transforming spirit.

Second Day
Matthew 28:18-20   Rite of rebirth.

Third Day
Luke 22:7-20   No greater gift.

Fourth Day
John 20:19-23   Channel of peace and reconciliation.

Fifth Day
James 5:13-16   Oil of strength.

Sixth Day
Mark 6:7-13   Commissioned to heal.

Seventh Day
Matthew 10:1-10   Extending the Lord's healing power.

Additional scripture readings:
Colossians 3:12-17, I Corinthians 13:4-7

V

"I Am..."

I Am the Light of the World-I

John 8:12

THE LIGHT PROMISED by the prophets became a reality in the person of Jesus. Rightfully he could say: "I am the light of the world." This truth not only gives us new insights into the person of Jesus, but it brings us the reassurance that if we follow him, our Light, we will never lose our way in this land of exile.

By his words and deeds Jesus reveals himself as the light of the world. His illuminating power issues from his divine nature: "the real light which gives light to every man coming into the world" (Jn 1:9).

Light in biblical language can either mean light which comes from the source of life, or the light which gives life. Both meanings are fulfilled in Jesus. Just as a flower will never bloom unless it is exposed to the sunlight, so our lives will never bear fruit unless we bask in the sunshine of the presence of Jesus, the light of the world.

Jesus guarantees us that if we follow him as the light of our life, we shall never stray, nor be lost. He says plainly: "No follower of mine shall ever walk in darkness; no, he shall possess the light of life." How comforting is such a generous promise!

At another time Jesus said: "I have come to the world as its light, to keep anyone who believes in me from remaining in the dark" (Jn 12:46). Jesus brings us into the light of his presence where he shares with us his divine life with its fruits of love, peace and joy, as a foretaste of our eternal union with him.

During his earthly sojourn, the divine light dwelling within Jesus was hidden under his humanity. On Mount Tabor that divine light was revealed. The words of the evangelist are revealing but inadequate: "His face became as dazzling as the sun, his clothes as radiant as light" (Mt 17:2).

This light was in anticipation of the glory of his risen state which he shares with us. It is "the glory of God shining on the face of Christ" (II Cor 4:6).

You Are the Light of the World

IN HIS PROPHETIC word Jesus said to us: "You are the light of the world" (Mt 5:14). Jesus fills us with his own divine life and light so that we can become channels of his life and light to all those he sends across our path. Time spent in prayer brings us to a more profound realization of the blessings which we enjoy and of our mission to diffuse his life and light to others.

First Day
John 3:16-21   *Love gives the greatest gift.*

Second Day
John 8:12   *The Light of the world.*

Third Day
John 9:1- 40   *Jesus reveals himself.*

Fourth Day
John 12:44-50   *Faith illumines acceptance.*

Fifth Day
Matthew 17:1- 8   *Radiance of the Son.*

Sixth Day
John 1:1-5   *Light dispels darkness.*

Seventh Day
II Corinthians 4:1-7   *The face of Christ.*

Additional scripture readings:
I John 1:5, Luke 1:78-79 and 2:29-32

I Am the Light of the World-II

John 9:1-41

JESUS CAME INTO the world as the light of the world. As we follow him in manifesting himself as the light of the world, we discover that Jesus frequently restored sight to the blind, bringing a new light into their lives.

We do not know how many Jesus cured of blindness. Repeatedly the evangelists record facts like this: "He restored sight to many who were blind" (Lk 7:21). Again: "He healed all who were in need of healing" (Lk 9:11).

Furthermore, Jesus not only conferred physical sight to the blind, but he brought them the light of faith, which is even more significant.

When Jesus healed the man born blind, he said: "While I am in the world, I am the light of the world." After some time Jesus also led this man into faith. The man healed of his blindness made a simple, but sincere act of faith: " 'I do believe, Lord,' he said, and bowed down to worship him."

Bartimaeus also manifested his faith in Jesus. He pleaded with Jesus to restore his sight: "Rabboni, I want to see." When the crowd tried to silence him, he shouted all the louder, "Son of David, have pity on me!" When Jesus rewarded his perseverance and restored his sight, he told Bartimaeus: "Your faith has healed you" (Mk 10:46-52).

Not only did those who were healed of their blindness believe in Jesus themselves, but they began to spread the good news of his loving compassion. They zealously tried to bring others into the light and life which Jesus came to impart.

Jesus also sternly warned those who might blind themselves to the message of the good news he came to proclaim. In reprimanding the Pharisees, calling them "blind guides," he was appealing to us to remain receptive to his word and to "walk while you have the light, keep faith in the light; thus you will become sons of light" (Jn 12:36).

Walk in the Light

AT TIMES OUR spiritual vision can be somewhat impaired by our humanness. We may not readily recognize that his thoughts are not always our thoughts, nor our ways his ways. With blind Bartimaeus we need to plead: "Lord, I want to see." Prayerfully listening will improve our spiritual focus so that we may more easily appreciate his caring, concerned and continuous love for us.

First Day
John 9:1-41   *Struggling for the light of faith.*

Second Day
Matthew 20:29-34   *Open our eyes.*

Third Day
Mark 10:46-52   *The healing power of faith.*

Fourth Day
Mark 8:22-26   *Gradual enlightenment.*

Fifth Day
Matthew 9:27-31   *Healed by faith.*

Sixth Day
Matthew 23:13-19   *A stern warning.*

Seventh Day
John 12:35-36   *Become sons of light!*

Additional scripture readings:
Tobit 11:9-15, I John 2:7-11, Psalm 146:1-10

I Am the Good Shepherd

John 10:1-18

THE IMAGE OF Jesus as the Good Shepherd is one of the better known and loved pictures of Jesus. It tells us so very much about him. The picture of a shepherd is woven into the language and imagery of the whole Bible. It speaks to us of God's providential care and also the loving concern of Jesus for each one of us, his sheep.

Jesus is the Good Shepherd because he is the Messiah. Repeatedly throughout the Old Testament and especially in the Psalms is the Messiah called a shepherd. Isaiah says: "Like a shepherd he feeds his flock; in his arms he gathers the lambs, carrying them in his bosom, and leading the ewes with care" (Is 40:11).

Jesus is the Good Shepherd who goes in search of the lost sheep. "And when he finds it, he puts it on his shoulders in jubilation" (Lk 15:5).

A shepherd's life is a hard life. It requires constant vigilance in protecting and guiding his sheep. It demands much patience in keeping the flock together and searching out good pasture. It is also a dangerous life. At times a shepherd may lose his life in protecting his sheep against robbers, or he may fall over one of the dangerous cliffs.

Jesus met all these requirements in caring for his flock; hence the title is most appropriate. Jesus provides for us spiritually: "I came that they might have life and have it to the full." As the Good Shepherd he is willing to lay down his life for us, his sheep: "for these sheep I will give my life." He gives himself freely because he loves us: "No one takes it from me: I lay it down freely." Jesus establishes an intimate, personal relationship with his sheep: "I know my sheep and my sheep know me. . . . My sheep hear my voice. I know them, and they follow me."

What comfort and what joy knowing that we are never alone, but we are always in the loving care of the Good Shepherd!

We Are the People He Shepherds

WHEN JESUS PORTRAYS himself as the Good Shepherd, he gives us so many insights into the mystery of his multi-faceted love for us. Jesus assured us that he came that we may have life to the full. The awareness of this superabundance of his love removes all tensions, worries and anxieties from our lives. In prayer let us listen to the Shepherd's voice.

First Day
Isaiah 40:1-11   *The Messiah is a shepherd.*

Second Day
Psalm 23:1-6   *His providential love is all-inclusive.*

Third Day
John 10:1-18   *He calls us by name.*

Fourth Day
Matthew 18:1-14   *Little lambs are precious.*

Fifth Day
Luke 12:32-34   *His little flock.*

Sixth Day
Mark 6:34-44   *A provident shepherd.*

Seventh Day
John 21:15-17   *The shepherd continues to tend his sheep.*

Additional scripture readings:
Hebrews 13:20-21, Psalm 95, Mark 14:27, Matthew 26:31, John 16:32

I Am the Way

John 14:6

JESUS DESCRIBES ONE phase of his ministry briefly but emphatically when he says: "I am the Way!" The ancient Semites were a nomadic people; hence the way, the route, the pathway was important to them. Jesus adapts himself to their vocabulary and to ours when he speaks of himself as the Way. Jesus is saying that the way is not a law, but a person. He is that Person.

Imagine yourself in a strange city, asking for directions. The directions you receive may only serve to confuse you even more or cause you to lose your way completely. On the other hand suppose that a person were to say to you: "Come, I will take you there." How enjoyable the journey and how delightful the destination would be.

Jesus does precisely that for us. He does not simply give us a series of directives, advice and laws to follow, but he says: "I am the Way, come I will go with you." He takes us by the hand, leads us, strengthens us and guides us personally each day.

Jesus assures us that he is the only way to the Father: "No one comes to the Father but through me." As he called the first disciples individually, so he calls each one of us: "Come, follow me."

Jesus does not deceive us, but tells us plainly the conditions for following him: "Whoever wishes to be my follower must deny his very self, take up his cross each day, and follow in my steps" (Lk 9:23).

Jesus shows us that the only way to glory is through the cross. The transfiguration on Mt. Tabor lights up the path leading to Calvary. Calvary is not the end. The cross is the doorway into the resurrection and the life which will be eternal.

Jesus did not point the way to the cross and bid us continue our journey alone. No, he said plainly: "I am the Way" and will lead you, support you, strengthen you and love you every step of the way.

Teach Me Your Ways, O Lord

IN MAKING A long journey, we must study the roadmap, provide food and drink for our sustenance and rest frequently to recover our strength. Jesus gave us the directives for our journey back to the Father, supplied us with food for the journey, and now bids us to rest frequently with him that he may renew and refresh us. Prayer is the process whereby we accomplish these ends.

First Day
Luke 3:3-6   The way of the Lord.

Second Day
Matthew 6:26-34   His way of holiness.

Third Day
Matthew 7:13-14   The wide and the narrow ways.

Fourth Day
Luke 9:57-62   Apostolic requirements.

Fifth Day
John 12:31-36   Walk in the light.

Sixth Day
John 14:1-7   How we can know the way.

Seventh Day
Ephesians 4:17-24   A new and fresh way.

Additional scripture readings:
II John 1:4-6, Psalm 25:1-22

I Am the Truth

John 14:6

A TEACHER MAY say to his students, ''I have taught you the truth;'' but only Jesus could say, ''I am the Truth.'' Truth in the biblical sense of the term is founded on a religious experience, an encounter with God. Now Jesus is the fullness of revelation, and he is God; hence he could honestly say, ''I am the Truth.''

Jesus identifies himself with the Father: ''The Father and I are one'' (Jn 10:30). Again Jesus states this truth: ''I am in the Father and the Father is in me'' (Jn 14:10f). In effect, Jesus is saying: ''If the Father is the Truth, then I also am the Truth, because the Father and I are one.''

Jesus insists on this title because he is the Word. He has come into the world to proclaim the Good News to us. The credibility of his Word is beyond any doubt.

Truth is both the Person of Jesus himself and also the Word he came to proclaim. Jesus makes this point because his Word should lead us to believe in him and believing in him will bring us eternal life.

Jesus did not merely give us the revelation of the Truth and then let us flounder to find our own way. He gave us the Holy Spirit as the Spirit of Truth. He promised: ''I will ask the Father and he will give you another Paraclete—to be with you always: the Spirit of Truth'' (Jn 14:16).

Jesus tells us furthermore that the fundamental office of the Spirit is to recall to our minds all that Jesus taught and to help us to grasp its true meaning in our lives today. ''The Holy Spirit . . . will instruct you in everything and remind you of all I told you'' (Jn 14:26).

Just as Jesus is identified with the Father, so he is also one with the Spirit. The Holy Spirit is the fullness of Jesus dwelling with us and within us.

For us, then, truth is the revealing Word of the Father, present in Jesus, illuminated by the Spirit. When we welcome this Word in faith, it will transform our lives.

The Truth Transforms

JESUS IS THE Truth which transforms our lives. Once we are transformed, Jesus asks us to be his disciples and teach the truth to others. A spiritual truth cannot be conveyed merely by words, but by example, by witnessing to that truth in our own lives. Time spent in prayer not only transforms our own lives, but helps us radiate the Truth itself.

First Day
Psalm 86:1-17   Walk in truth.

Second Day
John 8:31-32   Truth makes us free.

Third Day
John 4:21-24   A deeper worship.

Fourth Day
John 14:15-17   With you and within you.

Fifth Day
John 16:12-16   A divine guide.

Sixth Day
John 17:17-19   Consecrated by the truth.

Seventh Day
John 18:33-38   What does truth mean?

Additional scripture readings:
I Corinthians 13:4-7, I Timothy 2:1-8

I Am the Life

John 14:6

OUR LOVING AND living Father calls each one of us to eternal life. From the beginning to the end of the Bible, there is a profound appreciation of life in all its forms. These attitudes indicate that man hopefully and untiringly pursues life as a sacred gift from God.

When Jesus came upon the scene he stated clearly that he was not only the way to life, but that he was life itself: "I am the Life." Jesus also set forth the reason for his coming into the world. As the Good Shepherd he said: "I came that they might have life and have it to the full" (Jn 10:10).

Jesus proved that he is the master of all life. Jesus could not tolerate the presence of death, and he restored physical life to those who had already died. Furthermore, Jesus showed his power to give eternal life by proving his power over sin (Mt 9:1-7).

Sin alone can rob us of enjoying eternal life with him.

Jesus also promised that the life he would give would be an everlasting life. He plainly said: "I am the resurrection and the life." Jesus went on to say that in order to obtain this life, faith in him is required: "Whoever believes in me, though he should die, will come to life; and whoever is alive and believes in me will never die" (Jn 11:25f).

Jesus also laid down some conditions for obtaining divine life. One must follow the narrow path, "deny his very self, take up his cross, and begin to follow in my footsteps." He speaks paradoxically when he goes on to say: "Whoever would save his life will lose it, but whoever loses his life for my sake will find it" (Mt 16:24ff).

St. Paul explains to us that through our Baptism we die with Christ, but we are also raised with him to eternal life. In Baptism Jesus is already sharing with us the first stages of his divine life. With St. Paul we, too, can say: "The life I live now is not my own; Christ is living in me" (Gal 2:20).

A Divine Gift

THE PROMISE AND the gift of everlasting life surpass our wildest dreams. The recognition that Jesus is already sharing a portion of his divine life with us brings us much hope and great joy. Our contemplative prayer-posture will enable us to respond more deeply and more generously to his divine life and love.

First Day
John 10:10   No greater gift possible.

Second Day
John 4:10-14   Fountain of divine life.

Third Day
John 6:25-58   Daily source of eternal life.

Fourth Day
Matthew 16:24-28   Paradox of life after life.

Fifth Day
John 11:23-27   Life through resurrection.

Sixth Day
John 17:1-8   Gift of eternal life.

Seventh Day
Romans 6:3-11   From death to life.

Additional scripture readings:
I John 5:11-12, Luke 8:49-56, I Corinthians 15:1-58

I Myself Am the Bread of Life

John 6:35-40

JESUS LOVES US so much he wants to be a part of our lives, to share our mutual interests, our hopes and aspirations, our joys and sorrows. He wants to be with us to inspire us, to encourage us, to nourish us, and above all to love us.

He promised: "I will not leave you orphaned; I will come back to you" (Jn 14:18). In his parting words he encourages us with this reassurance: "Know that I am with you always, until the end of the world" (Mt 28:20).

Jesus is present with us and within us in his glorified, risen state. It is a very real presence, but a mysterious one. However, Jesus accommodates himself to our human limitations by giving us visible, tangible signs of his abiding presence in the Eucharist. The bread and wine are not meaningless signs. They are significant and symbolic. They speak to us of the essentials for our daily living—our food and our drink.

The manna in the desert manifests God's providential love. It was also a preparation for the gift of himself in the Eucharist. During his teaching ministry Jesus meticulously prepared us for this unique gift by changing water into wine and by feeding the multitudes.

Then he made his solemn promise to us nearly a year before the actual institution of the Holy Eucharist. "I myself am the bread of life." After that statement, Jesus told us of the fruits of his Eucharistic presence: "No one who comes to me shall ever thirst." What joy and reassurance this promise brings us. Jesus promises even more: "No one who comes will I ever reject." Only divine love could be so generous and gracious.

How eager Jesus was to give us this tremendous gift of himself! How he must have looked forward to that day in the Upper Room! He continues to say to us each day as he said to the apostles: "I have greatly desired to eat this Passover with you" (Lk 22:15).

Our Daily Bread

AS WE RECEIVE Jesus in the Eucharist, he will bless and consecrate us, condition and convert us, mold and transform us, so that we can radiate his love, peace and joy to others. In brief, Jesus became Eucharist for us so that we can become Eucharist to others. Our prayer will enrich this awareness and deepen our appreciation of this truth.

First Day
John 6:1-15   *Jesus prepares us for this gift.*

Second Day
Luke 22:14-20   *Listen to the desire of Jesus' heart.*

Third Day
John 6:25-33   *The Father's generosity.*

Fourth Day
John 6:35-40   *No more hunger, no more thirst.*

Fifth Day
John 6:44-58   *Promise of life.*

Sixth Day
John 6:60-61   *Pathetic rejection.*

Seventh Day
I Corinthians 11:17-34   *Recognize Jesus in the Eucharist.*

Additional scripture readings:
Exodus 16:4-15, Matthew 26:26-30

Do This in Remembrance of Me

Luke 22:14-20

JESUS WAS RATHER explicit and imperative in the instruction he gave us in the Upper Room: "Do this in remembrance of me." What did Jesus really mean by these words? Just before Jesus began the Passover meal, he gave us another directive: "What I just did was to give you an example: as I have done, so you must do" (Jn 13:15).

What did Jesus do? What is the example he wants us to follow? Jesus' life was one continuous and complete oblation to his Father from the moment of his conception until his last gasp on the cross. The paschal mystery was the formalization and the culmination of this giving of himself.

The sacrifices of the Old Testament did not remit sin. Jesus came to offer himself as the perfect sacrifice. This was all in God's plan and Jesus could say: "I have come to do your will, O God" (Heb 10:7).

In his promise of the Eucharist, Jesus said: "It is not to do my own will that I have come down from heaven, but to do the will of him who sent me" (Jn 6:38). Jesus was single-hearted in his determination to do exactly what the Father asked of him.

In proclaiming the Good News, Jesus taught precisely what the Father asked him to say: "For I have not spoken on my own; no, the Father who sent me has commanded me what to say and how to speak" (Jn 12:49).

Even in his darkest hour Jesus did not waver from his set purpose of doing the will of the Father. In his dreadful agony, Jesus could anticipate the full horror of his scourging and crucifixion, yet his prayer was one of total submission: "Father, if it is your will, take this cup from me; yet not my will but yours be done" (Lk 22:42). With his dying breath he reiterated his total submission: "Father, into your hands I commend my spirit" (Lk 23:46).

When Jesus says: "Do this in remembrance of me," he is asking us to give ourselves to the Father as unreservedly as he gave himself.

Our Daily Gift

EACH DAY AT Mass we enjoy the unique privilege of giving ourselves and all that we do to God through the hands of Jesus. Even though our gift may be half-hearted and self-centered, Jesus accepts it and unites it with the gift of himself. Thus he adds an infinite dimension to our gift and presents it to the Father in our name.

First Day
Luke 22:14-20   No greater gift possible.

Second Day
John 10:17-18   Given freely and willingly.

Third Day
John 12:44-50   The Father speaks.

Fourth Day
John 6:35-40   His will only.

Fifth Day
John 14:23-31   Word from the Father.

Sixth Day
Luke 22:39-46   The most crucial test.

Seventh Day
Luke 23:46   The final and total gift.

Additional scripture readings:
John 12:23-36, John 14:8-17, Matthew 11:25-27

I Am the True Vine

John 15:1-8

IN BEAUTIFUL PASTORAL imagery Jesus reveals to us the tremendous mystery of his divine indwelling. In the allegory of the Vine and Branches, Jesus teaches the sublime truth of his presence within us in his risen, exalted, glorified life.

This illustration is quite simple, but the truth it conveys is profound and beyond our comprehension. Jesus loved us so much he could not leave us. He wanted to remain with us and share in all our undertakings. His indwelling, however, is not static. It is a dynamic, operative presence without which we could do nothing. Did he not say: "Apart from me you can do nothing"?

This image is very apt because a vine needs much attention. The soil in which it grows must be prepared and cared for. The vine grows luxuriously, but some branches will never bear fruit. It needs constant pruning. It must be well watered and exposed to the warm sunshine. How perfectly this fits our own lives!

The goodness of our loving Father is also evident in the fact that it is the branch which blossoms out and bears the fruit, and Jesus tells us we are that branch. However, only with his divine life surging through us will we be able to bear fruit.

There is an even greater mystery contained in this pastoral illustration. It is the mystery of God's love. Jesus promised us: "I will not leave you orphaned; I will come back to you" (Jn 14:18). Before leaving us, he assured us: "And know that I am with you always, until the end of the world" (Mt 28:20).

What comfort and joy this brings us, knowing we, like the disciples on the road to Emmaus, are never alone. He is always with us, strengthening, nourishing, supporting, loving us.

With his abiding presence, we do become fruitful branches, and we do bring glory to God by the fruit we and Jesus produce. This is the foretaste of our total union with him in heaven.

The Glory of the Christian

WE ARE CHRISTIANS because Jesus is dwelling with us and within us. This mystery is so staggering that it is necessary for us to withdraw in solitude to contemplate its uniqueness. Our daily contact with Jesus in prayer will keep us aware of our great privilege, and also help us to penetrate a little more deeply its richness and beauty.

First Day
John 15:1-8   A mysterious allegory.

Second Day
Isaiah 27:1-7   The vineyard song.

Third Day
John 14:16-21   A unique dwelling place.

Fourth Day
Matthew 28:18-20   Never alone.

Fifth Day
John 1:10-14 -   His presence empowers.

Sixth Day
Luke 24:13-35   Our daily journey to Emmaus.

Seventh Day
II Corinthians 6:16-18   We are his people.

Additional scripture readings:
*John 14:23-26, I Corinthians 3:16-17; 6:19-20,
Matthew 1:18-25*

I Am the Messiah

John 4:19-25

JESUS CAME INTO the world to tell us who he is. We do have considerable theological knowledge about Jesus, but he wants us not merely to know more about him, but to know him as a Person.

One title which Jesus used very sparingly is that of Messiah. "Messiah", transliterated from the Hebrew, and "Christ", transcribed from the Greek, both mean "anointed." In apostolic times Jesus was called Christ as a proper name.

The contemporaries of Jesus had a false notion of the Messiah. They were expecting the Messiah to be a political leader who would free them from the domination of any foreign nation and reestablish the Davidic dynasty in all its pristine glory. This is the reason why Jesus would not let the demons call him the Messiah, because the Jews still did not have the true concept of the Messiah as the Savior and Redeemer.

When the angels announced his birth to the shepherds, they used the title of Messiah. "This day in David's city a savior has been born to you, the Messiah and Lord" (Lk 2:11).

Jesus did, however, accept this title of Messiah from Peter because the Apostle was beginning to understand its true meaning. When Jesus asked Peter: "And you, who do you say I am?" Peter's prompt reply was: "You are the Messiah, the Son of the living God!" Jesus not only accepted the title from Peter, but he went on to say to him: "No mere man has revealed this to you, but my heavenly Father" (Mt 16:15ff).

It is interesting to note that Jesus twice called himself the Messiah and both times under peculiar circumstances. The Samaritan woman said to Jesus: "I know there is a Messiah coming," and Jesus replied, "I who speak to you am he" (Jn 4:25f).

Secondly, when Jesus was being unjustly tried by the Sanhedrin, the high priest demanded: "Are you the Messiah, the Son of the Blessed One?" Jesus' answer could not have been more direct: "I am" (Mk 14:61f).

What joy and what consolation for us to know that Jesus is our Savior, the Messiah and Lord.

Messiah and Lord

JESUS CAME INTO the world to redeem us and unite us once again with our Father. However, there are many facets to his ministry, all of which merit a different title. We need to spend quiet time in listening in order to fathom the infinite love which reaches out to supply all our needs. Today let us rejoice in the knowledge that he is the Messiah.

First Day
Luke 2:8-19   Announcement from on high.

Second Day
John 1:35-51   The Messiah is found.

Third Day
John 4:21-30   Privileged message to a Samaritan.

Fourth Day
Matthew 16:13-17   Special inspiration.

Fifth Day
John 7:40-52   True concept of the Messiah.

Sixth Day
John 10:22-39   Faith requires listening.

Seventh Day
Mark 14:60-65   I am.

Additional scripture readings:
Luke 4:33-41, John 9:1ff, Mark 8:27-30

Jesus the King

John 18:33 - 19:16

FROM THE FIRSTV MOMENT OF HIS COMING INTO THE WORLD Jesus was called a king. The astrologers asked: "Where is the newborn king of the Jews?" (Mt 2:2). When Jesus called his first disciples, Nathanael exclaimed: "Rabbi, you are the king of Israel" (Jn 1:49). The prophets identified Jesus as a king: "Your king approaches you on a donkey's colt" (Jn 12:15).

Throughout the Gospel Jesus clearly and emphatically taught that he had come to establish his kingdom. However, it was not to be a political kingdom, as he told Pilate: "My kingdom does not belong to this world" (Jn 18:36).

The kingdom of Jesus is a spiritual kingdom. His kingdom is a mysterious reality which is revealed to the humble and little people, not to the learned and clever of this world (Mt 11:25f).

Jesus made the kingdom known to the disciples by means of a progressive revelation. It is a reign of love. Jesus told us of the great love the Father has for us: "Yes, God so loved the world that he gave his only Son" (Jn 3:16).

Jesus assures us that he loves us with that very same love: "As the Father has loved me, so I have loved you." He continues: "There is no greater love than this: to lay down one's life for one's friends" (Jn 15:9,13). By laying down his life for us he was able to make his dwelling within us by sharing his glorified, risen life with us. This is his kingdom, his reign of love.

Jesus laid down the conditions for establishing his kingdom within us: "Anyone who loves me will be true to my word, and my Father will love him; we will come to him and make our dwelling place with him" (Jn 14:23).

His indwelling gives us our true dignity. John the Baptist was one of the greatest, yet Jesus said: "I solemnly assure you, history has not known a man born of woman greater than John the Baptizer. Yet the least born into the Kingdom of God is greater than he" (Mt 11:11).

We are special people because Jesus is our king and we are members of his kingdom.

Our RSVP to a Royal Invitation

AS OUR KING, Jesus has invited and accepted us into his kingdom. One of the fruits of our membership in his kingdom is the outpouring of his life and love upon us. The only limitation on his gift is our ability to be open and our capacity to receive. That is why daily we pray: "Your kingdom come, your will be done."

First Day
Luke 14:15-24   Our personal invitation.

Second Day
Matthew 18:1-4   The ideal subject.

Third Day
Matthew 11:11-15   The least, but the greatest.

Fourth Day
Luke 12:32-34   Love does not fear.

Fifth Day
Luke 22:24-30   So humble a king.

Sixth Day
Matthew 25:31-46   A small gift, a great reward.

Seventh Day
Matthew 13:44-46   No more precious treasure.

Additional scripture readings:
Luke 23:35-43, Matthew 13:31-35, John 18:33-37, Matthew 6:9-13

I Am the Resurrection

John 11:25-26

MANY TIMES THROUGHOUT his earthly sojourn Jesus admonished us to be prepared for his coming at the time of our death and resurrection.

Jesus did not intend death to be a frightening experience, but rather the doorway into an eternal union of love with him. Our own resurrection began with our Baptism when we were given a share in the life of the Trinity. How comforting the teaching of St. Paul: "If we have been united with him through the likeness to his death, so shall we be through a like resurrection" (Rom 6:3-5).

Jesus promised us a resurrection when he said: "I solemnly assure you, the man who hears my word and has faith in him who sent me, possesses eternal life" (Jn 5:24). On another occasion he said that if we accept him, the Father will raise us up (Jn 6:40).

Jesus stated unequivocally that despite our physical death—the death of our animal life—we will live with him forever. "I am the resurrection and the life" (Jn 11:25-26). Jesus also said that he came into the world "that whoever believes in him may not die, but have eternal life" (Jn 3:16). And again: "I myself am the living bread come down from heaven. If anyone eats this bread he shall live forever" (Jn 6:51).

Often Jesus reminded us that he must die and rise so that he could share his divine life with us. Baptism is the source of that divine life. "The man who believes in it [the gospel] and accepts baptism will be saved" (Mk 16:16).

Jesus also taught us that our Baptism is the beginning of our own resurrection and that each day we must continue to die to self and surrender ourselves more completely to God in love.

Jesus was not concerned about imparting some facts about death and the life hereafter. He was primarily concerned in teaching us how to die to self each day and surrender more completely and more lovingly to the Father. This attitude guarantees our own glorious resurrection.

From Death to Life

AS WE CONTEMPLATE the teaching of Jesus about life here and hereafter, he will grant us special enlightenment if we are open to receive his Word. This enlightenment shows us the meaninglessness of worldly, self-centered values, and shows us the sheer joy of surrendering to God's holy will in all our decisions. Let us ask for that grace of enlightenment as we listen to Jesus.

First Day
John 3:1-8   Rebirth in the Spirit.

Second Day
John 5:19-30   A solemn promise of eternal life.

Third Day
John 6:44-51   Jesus is the living bread.

Fourth Day
Matthew 16:24-28   Paradox—cross leads to joy.

Fifth Day
John 12:24   Harvest of eternal life.

Sixth Day
John 11:25-26   Life even in death.

Seventh Day
Romans 6:3-5   A dying and rising.

Additional scripture readings:
Mark 10:32-34, Luke 24:46-49, Mark 16:14-15, Luke 21:29-36

VI

Jesus Redeems

Jesus Touches Sinners

Luke 19:1-10

JESUS WORE HIS heart on his sleeve. In his encounters with people, Jesus revealed the disposition of his loving heart. His encounter with Zacchaeus in Jericho is no exception.

Zacchaeus was a wealthy man, but a lonely outcast. As a tax collector he was hated and despised. However, he had heard that Jesus befriended sinners and tax collectors.

In his determination to see Jesus, he ran ahead of the crowd and climbed into a tree in order to get a good view.

The crowd was pressing upon Jesus and demanding all his time and attention. Nevertheless, Jesus turned from the crowd to reach out in love to this unhappy man. He gave his whole attention and time to Zacchaeus, even coming into his home to dine with him.

The loving touch of Jesus was powerful. Zacchaeus was not only instantly converted by the presence of Jesus, but he showed the crowd the sincerity of his conversion. He was willing to make restitution far greater than was required by the law.

Another tax collector, named Levi, was deeply touched by Jesus' outreach in love. He left everything to follow him (Lk 5:27-32).

The Samaritan woman experienced the loving concern of Jesus and immediately saw herself for what she was (Jn 4:4-42).

The sinful woman who braved the scornful looks of the diners in Simon the Pharisee's home touched the heart of Jesus. His compassionate love freed her from the shackles of her sins (Lk 7:36-50).

The loving heart of Jesus far outweighed the dictates of the law when the woman taken in adultery was led to him. Listen to his expression of mercy: "Nor do I condemn you. You may go. But from now on, avoid this sin" (Jn 8:1-11).

His compassionate love prompted Jesus to say: "It is mercy I desire and not sacrifice." On another occasion he said: "I have not come to invite the self-righteous to a change of heart, but sinners."

More Joy in Heaven

JESUS SAYS TO US: "Here I stand, knocking at the door." He wants us to open our hearts to receive the outpouring of his forgiving, healing, redeeming love. We bring him much joy when we are receptive to his redemptive work in us. As we contemplate his merciful love, our response will be more loving and more grateful.

First Day
Luke 19:1-10   No more welcome guest.

Second Day
Luke 5:27-32   A predilection for tax collectors.

Third Day
Luke 7:36-50   Simon surprised.

Fourth Day
John 4:4-42   Living water.

Fifth Day
John 8:1-11   Message written in sand.

Sixth Day
Mark 2:1-12   A total healing.

Seventh Day
Luke 23:39-43   He stole heaven.

Additional scripture readings:
John 5:1-15, Revelation 3:14-22

Shepherd and Savior

Luke 15:1-7

JESUS CAME INTO the world primarily as our Savior and Redeemer. This was the principal reason for the Incarnation. Everything else in his life hinged on this ministry.

In order to impress this mission upon us Jesus proved his great love and compassion in countless different ways. He wanted to show us that his mercy and forgiveness sprang from his infinite love.

To prove his love Jesus told us the parable of the lost sheep. What a touching parable of mercy and compassion. This is a picture which Jesus drew of his Father and ours. God is happy when a sinner returns to him, just as a shepherd is when he has found a lost sheep.

As a shepherd Jesus assures us that he will personally go in search of a lost sheep. Also, when he finds that strayed sheep he will lovingly and gently carry it back on his shoulders.

In order to appreciate Jesus' words we recall that many of the flocks in his day were communal flocks. There were two or three shepherds in charge. When it was time to go home, the shepherds returned with their flocks. However, if one sheep was lost, one of the shepherds would remain to search for it. The returning shepherds would inform the villagers of the lost sheep. The whole community would watch for the return of the shepherd with the lost sheep across his shoulder. When he returned, all the people would rejoice and give thanks to God.

And Jesus says: "I tell you, there will likewise be more joy in heaven over one repentant sinner than over ninety-nine righteous people who have no need to repent."

Your Sins Are Forgiven

JESUS LOVES US with a forgiving, healing and redeeming love. Intellectually we know that he forgives us, but we need to know it with our heart. As we spend time with him in prayer, that reassuring truth penetrates our whole being and brings us much peace.

First Day
Isaiah 53:3-12   *His redeeming love is foretold.*

Second Day
Matthew 1:18-25   *Identified as Savior.*

Third Day
John 1:29   *The sacrificial Lamb.*

Fourth Day
Luke 15:1-7   *How much joy have you caused?*

Fifth Day
John 10:25-30   *The Savior's reassuring hope.*

Sixth Day
Luke 23:34   *A dying prayer for us.*

Seventh Day
I Peter 2:19-25   *We are healed.*

Additional scripture readings:
Psalm 32, Ezekiel 16:1-63

Savior Until the End of Time

Luke 24:46-49

WE OFTEN THINK of the historical Jesus as coming into the world to redeem us. After his mission was accomplished, he set up certain guidelines and channels to dispense his mercy and loving compassion, but he himself is in his glory at the right hand of the Father.

We need to recall that the glory of Jesus is simply continuing his redemptive work among us. He is still the Good Shepherd who goes in search of the lost sheep. The Good Shepherd willingly lays down his life for his sheep.

This brings us to a new appreciation of the compassion and mercy of Jesus. We often are disappointed at our own weaknesses; we have a sense of guilt and disappointment in ourselves because we have sinned.

On the other hand Jesus continues to assure us that when we come with humility and sincerity it brings him much happiness to reach out in loving forgiveness. He is still the shepherd who says: "Rejoice with me because I have found my lost sheep" (Lk 15:6).

Yes, "Jesus Christ is the same yesterday, today and forever" (Heb 13:8). When we come to him with all our human failings and beg his merciful forgiveness and his healing, we bring him much joy because we are giving him an opportunity of being what he wants to be most—our Savior and Redeemer.

What joy and what reassurance this gives us, knowing that Jesus is always eager and anxious to forgive if we but turn to him with sorrow and loving trust.

Jesus was thinking about his ongoing redemptive work when he said: "All this I tell you that my joy may be yours and your joy may be complete" (Jn 15:11).

Our Savior Here and Now

WE KNOW THAT Jesus saved the world by dying for the sins of all mankind. However, we need to know that he has forgiven us personally. In our prayer we hear him assuring us that he loves us so much that he cannot but forgive us all our failings.

First Day
John 3:16   *What greater prize—eternal life.*

Second Day
Mark 2:1-12   *Jesus has the power to forgive, but Jesus asks for faith.*

Third Day
John 20:19-23   *Channel of merciful love.*

Fourth Day
Matthew 26:26-30   *Ongoing forgiveness.*

Fifth Day
Matthew 6:9-15   *The Father accepts your willingness to forgive.*

Sixth Day
Luke 15:11-32   *This is your Father.*

Seventh Day
Hosea 11:1-11   *A gracious, loving Father.*

Additional scripture readings:
Psalm 51, Isaiah 43:25

Last Discourse

John, Chapters 14-17

IN THE HALLOWED precincts of the Upper Room Jesus gathered with his disciples for his final discourse to them. This was a momentous occasion since they were all aware of the treacherous plots underway to eliminate Jesus.

On this memorable evening Jesus rose majestically above the intrigue, the hatred, the rejection. the denial, the betrayal which were threatening to engulf him. What a lasting legacy he gave in his final words to us, his loved ones.

In his final instruction, Jesus revealed his loving concern for each one of us. There was not one word of self-pity. There was no needless anxiety about the dreadful humiliation and the rejection which were enveloping him. Even though his own heart must have been heavy, Jesus thought only of others.

In the outpouring of his love, Jesus spoke words of hope and encouragement to us: "Do not let your hearts be troubled. Have faith in God and faith in me" (Jn 14:1). He prepared us for what lay ahead and assured us of his abiding presence with us: "If you find that the world hates you, know that it has hated me before you" (Jn 15:18ff).

The human heart craves peace, tranquillity and serenity. Jesus promised peace as his farewell gift to us: "My peace is my gift to you" (Jn 14:27).

Jesus also told us he loves us so much that he will never leave us orphans, but will remain with us in his risen life. He promised: "Anyone who loves me will be true to my word, and my Father will love him; we will come to him and make our dwelling place with him" (Jn 14:23). Can there be any greater gift?

What reassurance Jesus gives us of his unfailing love for us: "As the Father has loved me, so I have loved you." That means that Jesus' love for us is without limit. Then he encourages us: "Live on in my love" (Jn 15:9) and there we will find peace and joy.

Live On in My Love

AS WE REST quietly and peacefully in the presence of Jesus living within us in his risen life, and as we listen to the outpouring of his heart on this night of intrigue, we cannot help but respond generously, graciously and lovingly. As we open ourselves to the flood of his love, the prayer of Jesus will be fulfilled: "That they may be one, even as we are one, as you, Father, are in me, and I in you." This is the foretaste of heaven.

First Day
John 14:1-3   Faith makes us trusting.

Second Day
John 15:18-25   Jesus consoles.

Third Day
John 15:9-17   How much does Jesus love us?

Fourth Day
John 16:1-4   We are in Jesus' company.

Fifth Day
John 14:27-31   The gift of peace.

Sixth Day
John 17:9-19   Jesus prays for his disciples.

Seventh Day
John 16:20-28   Jesus will return.

Additional scripture readings:
Galatians 2:19-21, John 16:16, Acts 17:22-31

The Patient Jesus

Matthew 26:1 - 27:31

AS WE CONTEMPLATE the passion and death of Jesus, one of the facets of his divine personality which shines forth is his infinite patience. Amid the invectives, the insults, the derision, the physical abuse which he was made to endure, the inexhaustible patience of Jesus is glowingly manifested.

One definition of patience as found in the dictionary is "bearing pains and trials calmly without complaint." As he was unjustly accused before the Sanhedrin, "Jesus remained silent" (Mt 26:63). How aptly these words fit Jesus' disposition, for he accepted the perverse decision without a word of complaint.

Patience is also defined as "manifesting forbearance under provocation." Jesus did just that. The prophet speaks of Jesus in these words: "Though he was harshly treated, he submitted and opened not his mouth" (Is 53:7). As we contemplate the inhuman scourging and the cruel crowning with thorns, we marvel at the forbearance of Jesus under such vicious provocation.

Another definition describes patience as "steadfastness despite opposition, difficulty or adversity." Again Jesus displayed this kind of patience. Nothing daunted him as he proceeded along the Via Dolorosa. During his dreadful agony in the Garden of Gethsemane, Jesus prayed: "Father, if it is your will, take this cup from me; yet not my will but yours be done" (Lk 22:42). The Father confirmed his will by sending an angel to strengthen Jesus so that he could continue. After that, Jesus remained steadfast despite all the opposition, difficulty and adversity challenging him.

These various definitions of patience fit Jesus perfectly. Throughout his sufferings Jesus was a paragon of patience because he loved us with an infinite love. Love must give; and infinite love must give all. Only a loving person can be patient. St. Paul tells us that one of the components of love is patience. "Love is patient, love is kind" (I Cor 13:4).

Wait in Patience and Know that I Am God

BY HIS PATIENT endurance Jesus leads us along the road to love. Love teaches us to be patient with God, with others, and with ourselves. When we ponder the ongoing patience of Jesus with all our faults and failures, with all our short-sightedness and self-centeredness, then our response becomes more loving and more patient.

First Day
Isaiah 53:3-7   Patient as a lamb.

Second Day
Matthew 26:57-68   Silence bespeaks patience.

Third Day
Matthew 27:27-31   Patient endurance.

Fourth Day
Matthew 27:15-26   Personal rejection.

Fifth Day
Luke 23:26-31   Loving service and concern.

Sixth Day
Matthew 27:35-44   Not even in death.

Seventh Day
James 5:7-11   Patiently waiting.

Additional scripture readings:
I Timothy 1:12-18, Mark 15:21, Matthew 27:32

The Silent Jesus on Trial

Luke 22:54 - 23:25

AFTER JESUS WAS arrested, he was dragged before various so-called courts of justice. The God of heaven and earth, the Judge of the living and the dead, is to be accused, judged and condemned by his own creatures.

These trials were the most heinous miscarriages of justice that the world has ever known. All the machinations which the evil one could devise were at work. The ingenuity of man's sinful, depraved human nature spewed out in the hatred, the jealousy, the blasphemy, the invectives leveled at their innocent victim.

In the midst of all this perfidy, the noble, meek, strong, loving personality of Jesus stands out like a brilliant light radiating around the world.

For the most part Jesus is silent. He speaks only when necessity demands it, but never in self-defense. There are many reasons why Jesus did not speak. In the first place it was useless; he was already condemned. They would have twisted and turned his words against him. Secondly, his words would never have been heard. Their minds were closed.

The silence of Jesus speaks eloquently. It caused consternation among his accusers and so-called judges. "Herod questioned Jesus at considerable length but Jesus made no answer." He did not know how to handle the silence of Jesus, so "Herod and his guards then treated him with contempt and insults" (Lk 23:9-11).

In the mock performance before the Sanhedrin, Jesus answered only what was required. He spoke not one word in his own defense. Pilate, too, was surprised that "Jesus did not answer him on a single count" (Mt 27:14).

By his silence, Jesus was sitting in judgment on his accusers and his judges. His silence figuratively pointed an accusing finger at them, causing them to look at themselves.

Jesus did not keep silence maliciously. He was hoping their own sense of guilt might initiate a conversion. For us the silence of Jesus speaks.

Who Do You Say I Am?

WHILE WE DEPLORE the despicable rejection and condemnation of Jesus, it is possible that we may have rejected or condemned him in our own lives. Do we question the will of God in certain events in our life? Have we ever been angry at God because of the turn of events? Every sin is a refusal to love. Listen to Jesus' silence and let it speak to you. Jesus is always ready to accept our response in love.

First Day
John 5:16-18 *Persecution and rejection begin.*

Second Day
John 11:45-54 *Condemnation under way.*

Third Day
John 18:12-14 *The gloating of Annas.*

Fourth Day
Luke 22:63-71 *The perfidy of the Sanhedrin.*

Fifth Day
John 18:28-40 *The cowardice of Pilate.*

Sixth Day
Luke 23:6-12 *The vanity of Herod.*

Seventh Day
John 19:1-16 *The capitulation of Pilate.*

Additional scripture readings:
Psalm 22, I Peter 3:13-22, I Corinthians 4:6-13

Jesus Speaks His Final Words

Matthew 27   Luke 23   John 19

IN TIMES OF stress and suffering a person often reveals his or her true self. During his crucifixion Jesus showed us another facet of his loving heart.

His dying concern was not for himself, but for others. He was thinking of us and the generations to come. His will was perfectly in tune with that of his Father. He did not threaten his enemies, nor vow revenge, nor scream invectives. Rather he continued to reach out in love to them.

The moments of death are very sacred. We cherish and cling to the final words of a loved one. The last words of Jesus not only tell us much about him but they also bring us much peace and consolation. Even in his dying moments Jesus was reaching out in loving concern for all of us.

Listen to his compassionate, merciful, forgiving love as he prays for his enemies: "Father, forgive them; they do not know what they are doing" (Lk 23:34). These were his enemies he was praying for, excusing them and begging forgiveness for them.

The manifestation of his loving concern touched the criminal who was being executed next to him. Jesus perceived the moment of grace; he saw the disposition of his heart and promised him a nonstop flight into heaven: "I assure you: this day you will be with me in paradise" (Lk 23:43).

When Jesus said, "I am thirsty," he was telling us how much his heart was longing for our love in return for the boundless love he was pouring out upon us.

In giving us his last treasure, Jesus was again proving his love. He loved his Mother dearly. He provided for her by placing her under the care of the beloved disciple. There is much more contained in that gesture. Jesus was giving us his Mother as our very own. His body, the Church, needed not only a head, but also a heart. We cherish her as the Mother of the Church and also as the special gift of Jesus to us.

A Legacy of Love

AS WE PONDER these final words of Jesus, a transformation will take place within us. We will be moved to a greater spirit of gratitude for his redemptive love. As his words find a home in our hearts, our compassion for others, our brothers and sisters in Christ, will be augmented. Our love in response to his love will fill our hearts and reach out in loving concern for others. Listen to what Jesus is saying.

First Day

Luke 23:34   *"Father forgive them; they do not know what they are doing."*

Second Day

Luke 23:39-43   *"This day you will be with me in paradise."*

Third Day

Matthew 27:45-50   *"My God, my God, why have you forsaken me."*

Fourth Day

John 19:28-29   *"I am thirsty."*

Fifth Day

John 19:25-27   *"There is your mother."*

Sixth Day

Luke 23:44-46   *"Father, into your hands, I commend my spirit."*

Seventh Day

John 19:30   *"Now it is finished."*

Additional scripture readings:

Psalm 22, Psalm 31, John 10:17-18

VII

Jesus Lives

Living with the Risen Jesus

Luke 24:13-35

THE FATHER SAYS to us: "I know well the plans I have in mind for you, plans for your welfare, not for woe!" (Jer 29:11). Who could have imagined or comprehended that his divine plan included our adoption as his sons and daughters? In that adoption process Jesus comes to dwell with us and within us in his risen life.

What love must have prompted such a divine indwelling! What dignity is ours! How often and in how many ways Jesus attempted to explain this mystery. When he said to us, "I am the vine, you are the branches," he was trying to illustrate for our understanding his mysterious and abiding presence. This graphic picture gives us a better insight into this sublime truth.

On the road to Emmaus, Jesus gives us another assurance that he is always traveling with us as each one of us makes our daily journey to Emmaus.

Jesus is present with us in the Eucharist. He gives us tangible signs of his Eucharistic presence in the bread and wine. There are a number of parallels between the events on the road to Emmaus and the Eucharistic celebration. The penitential rite is foreshadowed when Jesus chided the disciples about their lack of faith: "What little sense you have! How slow you are to believe all that the prophets have announced!"

Jesus entered into a para-liturgy of the Word for them. "Beginning, then, with Moses and all the prophets, he interpreted for them every passage of Scripture which referred to him."

The disciples then readily recognized him in the breaking of the bread. The commission which we receive at the end of Mass to become Eucharist to others was exemplified by the disciples when they hurried back to Jerusalem to share the good news that Jesus was risen from the dead.

In his final commission to us to make disciples of all nations and to teach them to carry out everything he commanded us, Jesus gives us a lasting reassurance: "Know that I am with you always until the end of the world!"

I Am With You Always

OUR REAL DIGNITY arises from the truth that we are "the temples of the living God" because Jesus is dwelling in us. Our problem is to keep ourselves ever aware of his abiding presence. As we spend time basking in his presence we can say with St. Paul: "In him we live and move and have our being." Then with the apostle we can also say: "The life I live now is not my own; Christ is living in me."

First Day
John 1:14-16   *We have a share in his fullness.*

Second Day
John 16:17-28   *How long is a short time?*

Third Day
John 14:18   *No orphans here.*

Fourth Day
Matthew 25:31-46   *Jesus is hungry and thirsty.*

Fifth Day
Luke 24:13-35   *Keeping our hearts burning within us.*

Sixth Day
Matthew 28:18-20   *A great legacy.*

Seventh Day
Revelation 3:20-22   *The latch string is on the inside.*

Additional scripture readings:
Galatians 2:19-21, John 16:16, Acts 17:22-31

Look at Jesus

John 1:35-51

BEFORE JESUS BEGAN his public ministry and before he launched out on his teaching mission, he went to the River Jordan to be baptized by John. John had consistently maintained that he was not the Promised One, but only a "herald's voice in the desert." It was John's privilege to present Jesus to a waiting world. He did so with a simple, direct and powerful declaration: "Look! There is the Lamb of God!" (Jn 1:36).

When John said, "Look," he did not mean a casual glance making us aware of the physical presence of Jesus nor a brief scrutiny of his physical appearance in order to be able to recognize him. No, John meant that we should behold, observe, study, reflect on who Jesus is and what he is. Furthermore, John wanted us to recognize the personality of Jesus as it was reflected by his actions and attitudes at the River Jordan. Here the Father also bade us to look at his Son as he was about to begin his teaching ministry.

Pilate unwittingly also invited us to concentrate on Jesus as he entered into the final stages of his redemptive ministry. Little did Pilate realize that his presentation of Jesus, after he had been scourged and crowned with thorns, was not only to the crowd of his enemies, but to the whole world for all ages to come. How his words reechoed down through the centuries: "Look at the man!" (Jn 19:5).

Our look in life must always be fixed on Jesus. Jesus wants to be the source of inspiration and motivation in our lives. He wants us to gaze at him with the eyes of faith. Jesus wants us to be aware of his indwelling permeating us with his risen, glorified, exalted life.

We need to look at Jesus to remember that he loves us with an infinite love. We need to look at Jesus to recall that he is so genuinely interested in us that he is aware of every hair that falls from our head.

Contemplative prayer is taking a long, loving look. Such a gaze has a transforming power. It is prayer at its best.

Gazing on the Lord

WHEN WE LOOK appreciatively and prayerfully upon Jesus as he begins his teaching mission of bringing the Good News, when we contemplate Jesus as the Man of Sorrows, then the mystery of divine love begins to unfold. Then our looking becomes loving in response to his overwhelming love.

First Day
John 1:29-34   *The long-awaited moment of the ages.*

Second Day
John 1:35-51   *You've got to see this for yourself.*

Third Day
Matthew 11:2-6   *Seeing is believing.*

Fourth Day
Luke 9:28-36   *Divine radiance.*

Fifth Day
John 19:4-16   *A pitiable, but powerful sight.*

Sixth Day
II Corinthians 3:18   *A transforming gaze.*

Seventh Day
II Corinthians 4:16-18   *Looking in the right direction.*

Additional scripture readings:
Luke 3:21-22, Matthew 3:13-17, Psalm 145, esp. v. 15,
Psalm 34, Matthew 18:10-14

Listen to Jesus

Matthew 13:1-23

AT THE THEOPHANY on Mt. Tabor, the Father himself urged us to listen to Jesus. "This is my Son, my Chosen One, listen to him" (Lk 9:35). This same admonition is found repeatedly throughout Sacred Scripture. Its frequent occurrence impresses upon us how important and how essential it is that we learn to listen.

We hear so very much. All day long our ears are bombarded with sounds and noises of all descriptions. We have learned to hear without listening. We listen so seldom.

Listening is an art. Listening means forgetting ourselves completely and placing ourselves into the position of the other person. We must strive to experience what he or she is experiencing, to feel as he or she does, to see everything through the other person's eyes, through his or her frame of reference. Jesus was a perfect listener. He had no hang-ups, no self-centered projects and programs.

Listening is vital because we cannot love a person to whom we have not listened. We cannot love God until we have learned to listen to him with every fiber of our being.

Listening is never artificial or stilted. It is warm, personal, interested, concerned. It seeks to know and to care.

Listening does not cause tension or anxiety lest we miss some important message. Listening means being totally receptive to the inspiration, to the presence, and to the love which Jesus is pouring out upon us.

Listening is love in action. Listening is praying. As we listen we penetrate through our human ego, permitting our spirit to get in touch with the Spirit of God who dwells in our heart. Quiet listening is experiencing God. Listening is communing with the mystery of God.

Listening is Loving

IN THE PARABLE of the sower Jesus is begging us to receive his word. To receive means to listen with our whole being. We cannot love a person we do not know. We cannot know a person to whom we have not listened. Jesus invites us to listen so that we might learn to know him more personally and to be able to respond more fully to the outpouring of his love upon us.

First Day
Isaiah 55:10-12   *The word will achieve its end.*

Second Day
John 1:1-5   *Who is the Word?*

Third Day
John 14:23-24   *To love is to obey.*

Fourth Day
Luke 11:27-28   *Genuine blessedness.*

Fifth Day
John 15:3   *Healing power in a word.*

Sixth Day
James 1:16-25   *Good listening.*

Seventh Day
I Peter 1:22-25   *The word is living and enduring.*

Additional scripture readings:
Psalm 119:105-112, Colossians 3:12-17, Romans 10:8-17, Hebrews 4:12-13

Long for Jesus

John 17:20-26

AT TIMES WE must pause to examine prayerfully certain attitudes which could influence our spiritual maturation. We must honestly and sincerely ask ourselves how well we want to know Jesus? Do we really want to form a deep personal relationship with him? Are we willing to die to self so that we may surrender more completely to him in love? Do we hesitate at times for fear that Jesus might ask too much? Are we like the rich man in the Gospel who went away sad?

Jesus is always a gentleman. He never imposes himself upon us. He is very solicitous that our own will remains free, even though he longs to unite us more closely with him. He wants us to come to him of our own volition, to long for a deeper union of mind and heart with him.

Jesus reveals his own love for us regardless of our attitudes. In Capernaum when he tried to prepare his hearers for the gift of himself in the Eucharist, "many of his disciples broke away and would not remain in his company any longer." Try to experience the anguish of Jesus as he said to the Twelve: "Do you want to leave me too?" (Jn 6:66).

Even to the man who had been sick for thirty-eight years Jesus first asked: "Do you want to be healed?" (Jn 5:6).

Jesus is eagerly awaiting us. He tells us: "Here I stand, knocking at the door" (Rev 3:20). And we remember that the latch string is on the inside.

The very desire for a more personal relationship with Jesus is a special grace. St. Paul says: "It is God who, in his good will toward you, begets in you any measure of desire or achievement" (Phil 3:13). Let us ask and desire that gift, "good measure pressed down, shaken together, running over."

Jesus alone can satisfy the longing of our hearts with his divine life and love. Did he not invite us: "If anyone thirsts, let him come to me" (Jn 7:37). He promised "living water" which alone can slack our thirst. Long for him and he will be faithful to his promise.

Even the Desire Is God's Gift

DO WE LONG for a deeper commitment to Jesus, but lack the generosity and trust to yield willingly and enthusiastically to him? That feeling arises in our unredeemed human nature. However, as we listen to the yearning of his heart, our love response comes more easily and more graciously.

First Day
Mark 10:17-27   Too great a price.

Second Day
John 4:4-26   Living water alone can quench our thirst.

Third Day
John 5:1-15   We must have a desire to be healed.

Fourth Day
John 7:37-39   A desire is based on faith.

Fifth Day
John 6:25-40   He alone will satisfy our hunger and thirst.

Sixth Day
Revelation 3:20-22   The latch-string is on the inside.

Seventh Day
Philippians 2:13   Ours for the asking.

Additional scripture readings:
Luke 22:15, Psalm 63, Psalm 42

Linger with Jesus

Luke 10:38-42

WE ENJOY BEING in the company of those who we love. We treasure each other's friendship and love. Such relationships are free and easy. Our being together is unplanned and unstructured. We can easily relax with those who are near and dear to us. We can be ourselves.

Jesus invites us to come aside to linger with him, to rest in the sunshine of his presence because he loves us and wants to be close to us. Like the rays of the sun, his presence warms us, cheers us, nourishes us, encourages and strengthens us.

Linger with Jesus as he invites his disciples and you to "come by yourselves to an out-of-the-way place and rest a little" (Mk 6:31). The disciples had just returned from a busy mission of preaching the need of repentance and healing the afflicted. Jesus wanted them to linger with him and to ponder what God had done through them.

Jesus knows how busy our lives can become so that, like the disciples, we hardly have time to eat. He knows, furthermore, that life can become routine, monotonous and even discouraging at times; that is why he invites us to linger with him: "Come to me, all you who are weary and find life burdensome, and I will refresh you" (Mt 11:28).

Jesus invites us to become his disciples. A disciple is a person who follows the master. He or she lingers with the master to observe his mentality and attitudes. The disciple learns not so much by a lecture-style teaching, but mostly by observing. By lingering with the master, he or she begins to imitate him.

When Jesus invited the disciples of John the Baptist to "come and see," it was not merely to see the place of his lodging; rather they were to linger with him to discover his way of life and his teaching. Some think that this was the eve of the sabbath and that they stayed for a considerable time with Jesus.

Jesus invites us to linger with him.

Come and See

LINGER IN PRAYER with Jesus on the Mount of the Beatitudes as he explains his way of life. Linger with him as he manifests his divine love in healing all who come to him. Linger with him as he tells you how very much he loves you.

First Day
Luke 10:38-42   *Mary lingered.*

Second Day
Mark 6:30-32   *Linger with Jesus in solitude.*

Third Day
Matthew 11:28   *Linger with Jesus when you are weary.*

Fourth Day
John 1:35-51   *To follow means to linger with.*

Fifth Day
Matthew 9:9-13   *Levi responded and lingered.*

Sixth Day
Mark 10:17-31   *A good man who did not linger.*

Seventh Day
Luke 22:39-46   *An invitation to linger and pray.*

Additional scripture readings:
Isaiah 55:1-13, John 4:39-42, John 15:7-8

Learn from Jesus

John 14:6-7

AN EAGER DISCIPLE learns much from his master. He is not so much concerned about acquiring more information, new ideas or deeper insights, as he is concerned about permitting the Master's way of life to mold and transform him.

The words, attitudes, actions and way of life of Jesus have a tremendous transforming power as we open ourselves to their influence. Jesus' invitation is direct: "Learn from me."

Jesus instructs us by his word. His word is always replete with guidelines which lead us to a more personal relationship with him. In the Beatitudes, Jesus is leading us to a new way of life. In effect, he is saying that this is the standard of living he is proposing, and blessed will be his disciples who strive to live by this standard. "If you live according to my teaching, you are truly my disciples" (Jn 8:31).

Jesus showed us how to love. His concern for the sick and suffering teaches us how we ought to love. Suffering was considered a punishment from God; thus it was not regarded as noble and praiseworthy to love the afflicted as Jesus did.

Associating with sinners was also a taboo in his day. His compassionate heart touched many sinners who turned to God because he went out to them in love, even though he was criticized for this: "This man welcomes sinners and eats with them" (Lk 15:2).

Jesus also teaches us how to pray not only by his word, but by his own example. "He went out to the mountain to pray" (Lk 6:12). He also prayed publicly, "entering the synagogue on the sabbath as he was in the habit of doing" (Lk 4:16).

Jesus' whole way of life calls for our emulation, and he invites us to learn from him as he said: "I am the way, and the truth and the life; no one comes to the Father, but through me" (Jn 14:6).

Learn from Me

JESUS NEVER ASKS us to do anything which he himself has not already done. Gradually Jesus leads and encourages us to "put on the new man" and to "be transformed by the renewal of our mind." As we prayerfully listen, at the core of our being that transformation is taking place. Beg Jesus to give you a listening heart.

First Day
Luke 6:27-49   *To love*

Second Day
Luke 11:1-13   *To pray*

Third Day
Luke 18:9-14   *To be humble*

Fourth Day
Matthew 18:21-35   *To be forgiving*

Fifth Day
Luke 12:22-31   *To trust*

Sixth Day
Matthew 25:31-46   *To be generous*

Seventh Day
John 15:9-12   *To be joyous*

Additional scripture readings:
John 13:1-17, Matthew 23:1-12, John 13:34-35

Lean on Jesus

Luke 9:10-17

A FRIEND OF mine has coined an expression which he uses frequently: "Fear not, you are inadequate." This axiom leads us into an ideal prayer-posture. It reminds us of our complete dependence on God. Did not Jesus say: "Apart from me you can do nothing" (Jn 15:5)? This is just another way of saying that with Jesus we can accomplish all things.

This is a hard lesson for us to learn, since we pride ourselves on our self-sufficiency. We are living in an age of technology which relegates God to the realm of convenience, if it does not eliminate him altogether.

Jesus wants us to recognize our dependence upon him. Before he fed the crowd in an out-of-the-way place, he first asked his apostles: "Why do you not give them something to eat yourselves?" It was only when they acknowledged their helplessness and offered their small portion of five loaves and two fish, that Jesus multiplied their gift to feed the whole crowd.

On another occasion, toward the end of his discourse in which he promised to give us himself in the Holy Eucharist, when the crowds left him, Peter voiced loving trust and faith in Jesus: "Lord, to whom shall we go? You have the words of eternal life" (Jn 6:68).

Martha had great confidence in Jesus: "Lord, if you had been here, my brother would never have died" (Jn 11:21). The father of the possessed boy recognized his dependence on Jesus: "I do believe! Help my lack of trust" (Mk 9:24).

Jesus invites us: "Come to me, all you who are weary and find life burdensome" (Mt 11:28). Again he promises: "Ask and you shall receive" (Lk 11:9).

Consider the assurance he gave the criminal on the cross: "I assure you: this day you will be with me in paradise" (Lk 23:43).

Jesus wants to be equally generous with us, if we but lean on him.

Promise and Fulfillment

IN OUR PRAYER Jesus not only shows us our own inadequacy and our own inability to accomplish anything ourselves, but he also promises us all the help we need if we come to him with a spirit of poverty, with confidence and trust. Ask for that grace as you meet Jesus in these events.

First Day
Exodus 17:8-13   *Graphic picture of perseverance.*

Second Day
John 15:5   *With him we can do all things.*

Third Day
Luke 11:9-13   *Jesus gives us reassurance.*

Fourth Day
Luke 9:10-17   *Sharing a lunch.*

Fifth Day
John 6:66-69   *There is no other.*

Sixth Day
Mark 9:14-29   *A plea for faith and trust.*

Seventh Day
Luke 23:39-43   *A hopeful plea and solemn promise.*

Additional scripture readings:
John 11:1-44, Matthew 11:28-30, II Corinthians 12:7-10

Live in Jesus

John 15:1-8

AT THE LAST Supper there were many sentiments which filled the heart of Jesus. He gave expression to some of these thoughts in those touching words: "I have greatly desired to eat this Passover with you before I suffer" (Lk 22:15).

Jesus did not want to leave us orphans. He gave us tangible evidence of his abiding with us and within us by remaining with us in his sacramental presence. He continues to fill us with his divine life and love.

There is something mysterious about a divine presence. To help us appreciate this mystery, Jesus accommodated himself to our human limitations when he set forth this truth in a simple, picturesque allegory. How simple the words, but how profound the truth: "I am the vine, you are the branches."

In this brief but lucid metaphor Jesus reveals many truths. He tells us of the goodness of the Father in permitting us, the branches, to blossom out and bear fruit. He assures us that apart from him we can do nothing, which is just another way of saying that with him living in us we can do all things.

With these words, he encourages us to respond to his presence: "Live on in me, as I do in you." He continues to live in us that his word may purify us: "You are clean already, thanks to the word I have spoken to you."

Earlier in that same discourse in the Upper Room, Jesus told us how this divine indwelling can be effected: "Anyone who loves me will be true to my word, and my Father will love him; we will come to him and make our dwelling place with him" (Jn 14:23).

Toward the end of this discourse, Jesus prayed that his indwelling might be effected. He prayed: "That all may be one as you, Father, are in me, and I in you; I pray that they may be one in us" (Jn 17:21).

Jesus wants us to live in him so that he might accompany us at every moment of our earthly pilgrimage.

Love Is a Warming Mystery

WHAT PROFOUND MYSTERY is divine love! Jesus loves us so much he wants to remain with us and within us in his glorified, exalted, resurrected life. As we experience the warmth of his love at the core of our being, we will be enabled to respond to his over-whelming love in our own feeble way. Prayer will lead us into that mystery.

First Day
Exodus 40:34-38   The Lord is present.

Second Day
John 1:10-16   His presence empowers us.

Third Day
John 15:1-8   The vineyard of the Lord.

Fourth Day
John 14:23-26   Trinitarian indwelling.

Fifth Day
John 17:20-23   The prayer of Jesus is always heard.

Sixth Day
John 14:18-21   We are never alone.

Seventh Day
I Corinthians 3:16-17   Holy temples.

Additional scripture readings:
*Isaiah 5:1-7, Galatians 2:15-21, Ephesians 2:19-22,
I John 4:7-21*

Love Jesus

Matthew 25:31-46

AFTER THE RESURRECTION Jesus asked Peter a rather pointed and personal question: "Simon, son of John, do you love me?" (Jn 21:16). Three times Jesus asked this question to give Peter an opportunity to ponder well his response.

Jesus asks us that same question: "Do you really love me?" With Peter we strive to reply: "Lord, you know everything, you know I am trying to love you."

Jesus assures us that we are loved both by him and by his heavenly Father. "As the Father has loved me, so I have loved you. Live on in my love" (Jn 15:9). Jesus not only assures us of the infinite love with which the Father loves us, but he also reminds us that his own love is equally great. He then encourages us to receive and respond to this love: "Live on in my love."

We live in Jesus' love and we love him by spending time with him in prayer, especially the prayer of listening to the outpouring of his heart and by permitting him to love us. In prayer we are giving him the only gift he really wants—the gift of ourselves.

Repeatedly Jesus taught us how to love him: "If you love me keep my commandments." He showed us how to love not only by keeping his Father's commandments, but by fulfilling even the slightest wish of his Father. Furthermore, he proved his love by pouring out his very life's blood.

Jesus also instructed us that when we reach out in love to others, we are really loving him. Did he not say: "I assure you, as often as you did it for one of my least brothers, you did it for me."

After washing the feet of his apostles Jesus told them: "As I have done, so you must do." Then he went on to say: "I give you a new commandment: love one another. Such as my love has been for you so must your love be for each other" (Jn 13:15, 34).

Praying Is Loving

WE MIGHT FIND loving difficult at times. Jesus invites us to experience his love so that we can become a channel through which he can reach out in love to others. Jesus gradually leads us to four different levels of love. As we spend time in prayer we will find much joy in making the transition from one step to another.

First Day
Mark 12:31   *First level—as you love yourself.*

Second Day
Matthew 25:31- 46   *Second level—as you love me.*

Third Day
John 13:34-35   *Third level—a new commandment.*

Fourth Day
John 17:20-23   *Fourth level—united in love.*

Fifth Day
John 14:15-21   *Pleasing the beloved.*

Sixth Day
John 15:9-10   *No greater gift.*

Seventh Day
John 14:23-24   *Dwelling in love.*

Additional scripture readings:
John 13:1-17, Luke 10:25-37, I John 4:7-21

Let Jesus Love You

John 15:9-17

THE THEME OF this week's prayer, "Let Jesus Love You," should be an exciting and delightful experience. However, we may discover that we are hesitant about accepting the love God wants to pour out upon us. There are many reasons for this attitude.

Somehow we feel that we do not deserve to be loved by God because we have sinned so often. Secondly, we may feel that it is necessary for us to earn God's love by doing something special for him.

Both of these attitudes are understandable since most of us have a low self-esteem and also because we live in a culture which is production oriented. Nonetheless, our willingness to accept God's love is a crucial transition in our spiritual maturation.

Our Father has frequently told us that he loves us regardless of who we are or what we have done. He tells us that we are precious in his sight and glorious and he loves us (Is 43:1-5). He cares about even the slightest detail of our lives (Ps 139).

St. John also emphasizes the point that God loves us as we are: "Love, then, consists in this: not that we have loved God, but that he has loved us" (I Jn 4:10).

Jesus tries to convince us how much he loves us: "There is no greater love than this: to lay down one's life for one's friends." Jesus does exactly that for us willingly: "The Father loves me for this: that I lay down my life to take it up again" (Jn 10:17).

Jesus also assures us that the reason for his coming into the world was to share his divine life with us. "I came that they might have life and have it to the full" (Jn 10:10).

Jesus rose from the dead so that he could share his risen life with us even now on our earthly sojourn. Listen how fervently Jesus is praying for that redemptive action to take place within us: "That all may be one as you, Father, are in me, and I in You: I pray that they may be one in us. That they may be one, as we are one—I living in them, you living in me" (Jn 17:21ff).

Bathed in Love

CONTEMPLATIVE PRAYER IS like basking in the warm sunshine of God's loving presence. Just as the sun brightens our day, as it nourishes and warms us, so does the gentle love of God envelop us. As we bask in the sunshine of his love, absorbing its life-giving elements, enjoying its warmth, rejoicing in its light, we are permitting God to love us. And that love is a touch of heaven.

First Day

Isaiah 43:1-5 *We are precious because God loves us.*

Second Day

John 15:9-17 *How much does Jesus love us?*

Third Day

John 10:10 *The gift of life.*

Fourth Day

John 10:17-18 *Love knows no limit.*

Fifth Day

John 3:16 *Love gives eternal life.*

Sixth Day

I John 4:7-21 *Who loved first?*

Seventh Day

John 17:20-26 *Love seeks union.*

Additional scripture readings:

Psalm 139, Jeremiah 29:11-14, Matthew 6:25-34